IMPORTANT INFORMATION

Photocopying permission

The right to photocopy material in *Not Sunday, Not School!* is granted for the pages that contain the photocopying clause: 'Reproduced with permission from *Not Sunday, Not School!* published by BRF 2006 (1 84101 4907)', so long as reproduction is for use in a teaching situation by the original purchaser. The right to photocopy material is not granted for anyone other than the original purchaser without written permission from BRF.

The Copyright Licensing Agency (CLA)

If you are resident in the UK and you have a photocopying licence with the Copyright Licensing Agency (CLA), please check the terms of your licence. If your photocopying request falls within the terms of your licence, you may proceed without seeking further permission. If your request exceeds the terms of your CLA licence, please contact the CLA directly with your request. Copyright Licensing Agency, 90 Tottenham Court Rd, London W1T 4LP. Tel 020 7631 5555; fax 020 7631 5500; email cla@cla.co.uk; web www.cla.co.uk. The CLA will provide photocopying authorization and royalty fee information on behalf of BRF.

BRF is a Registered Charity (No. 233280)

Text copyright © Eleanor Zuercher 2006
Illustrations copyright © Paula Doherty 2006
The author asserts the moral right
to be identified as the author of this work

Published by
The Bible Reading Fellowship
First Floor, Elsfield Hall
15–17 Elsfield Way, Oxford OX2 8FG
Website: www.brf.org.uk

ISBN 1 84101 490 7
ISBN-13 978 1 8411 490 6
First published 2006
10 9 8 7 6 5 4 3 2 1 0

Acknowledgments
Scripture quotations are taken from the Contemporary English Version
of the Bible published by HarperCollins Publishers, copyright © 1991,
1992, 1995 American Bible Society.

A catalogue record for this book is available from the British Library

Printed in Singapore by Craft Print International Ltd

NOT SUNDAY NOT SCHOOL!

Through-the-year children's programmes
for small churches

Eleanor Zuercher

Eleanor Zuercher was by profession a chartered secretary, but has given up her job as company secretary with a firm of city solicitors in order to train as a teacher—which she suspects may be her true vocation! Eleanor lives and works in a rural parish in the West Buckingham Benefice (a group of six rural parishes) where, for the past four years, she has been running workshops for children aged 3–12. Alongside this work she oversees all the children's work for her parish as well as being involved in planning and taking services, taking school assemblies and occasional RE lessons, liaising between the church and the local infants school and developing other links with the local community. Eleanor has also undertaken a number of training courses, most recently *Leading Children*, a correspondence course run by St John's Extension Studies. The rural affairs magazine *Country Way* published a feature on her work in 2004.

For Crispin and Bertie, who inspired this book;
for Viv, Liz and Margaret, who encouraged it;
and for Hanno, who cheerfully tolerated it.

ACKNOWLEDGMENTS

My particular thanks go to the children of Acorns and Saplings, their families and especially the volunteer helpers and congregations of St Mary Magdalene in Tingewick and the rest of the West Buckingham Benefice, who all humoured me.

You encompass me behind and before:
and lay your hand upon me.
(Psalm 139:5)

CONTENTS

FOREWORD

When I first came across Eleanor Zuercher and her work during 2004, it was inspiring and exciting to learn about what had been achieved in a very difficult situation. Six rural congregations in a benefice in Buckinghamshire, with small numbers of adults and children, may seem to be an unpromising place to start a new children's initiative, but *Not Sunday, Not School!* proves otherwise.

The aim of *Country Way* magazine, which I edit, is to share ideas, information and inspiration on good rural church projects. The story of Acorns and Saplings shone out as a really good project that others could learn from and apply to their own situation. So this wonderful resource book, produced from tried and tested workshops and activities, will allow others to gain from the experiences and lessons learned.

In our changing times it is perhaps unrealistic to expect families to bring children to church early on Sunday mornings, with sports clubs and other activities often taking place at the time when Sunday school was traditionally scheduled. The approach suggested here challenges us to leave this model behind and offers interesting and worthwhile alternatives that will attract children and adults alike. This approach also offers hope to rural churches in large benefices and teams, proving that it is possible to manage and run meaningful and appropriate children's activities.

With books and resources such as this, small and rural churches have the seeds of hope for a lively and engaging future. Above all else, have fun in using and developing this practical and enthusing material!

Dr Jill Hopkinson
National Rural Officer for the Church of England

HOW TO USE THIS BOOK

This book contains thematic programmes for the Christian year, plus additional material for times of the year when there are no major festivals to celebrate. Each programme contains:

* ☆ Suggestions for Bible stories based on the theme
* ☆ Suggestions for creating a display for the church
* ☆ Craft activities
* ☆ Games
* ☆ Suggestions for prayer

Alongside the ten themes for the Christian year, on our website www.barnabasinchurches.org.uk you will find timed workshop plans, as well as ideas to assist you in integrating your children's work into the life of the church and, perhaps more importantly, integrating the regular congregation into the children's work. This is especially important if your children meet at a time other than Sunday morning, in which case there is a danger that they may become less visible to the rest of the congregation. Children and their families are a part of the congregation and whether they come to church on a Saturday, Sunday or any other day of the week should make no difference. However, if the PCC or governing body of your church is made up almost entirely of people who worship on a Sunday morning, work that takes place 'off the radar' can be easily overlooked.

The workshop plans on the website provide pick-and-mix ideas for you to use as a basis for creating your own programme. The timings given are guidelines only. You may find that activities will take much longer, or much less time. A lot will depend on the age of the children, their ability to concentrate, and how much they like the type of activity on offer. There are suggestions in the workshop plans for running activities simultaneously, whereby the children are split into two or three groups and rotate from one activity to the next. This could be helpful if time and space round the tables is restricted.

All additional material is available to download free of charge.

INTRODUCTION

The material in this book has been developed in the context of the rural church. Therefore the ideas and perceptions are un-apologetically from a rural perspective and rooted in particular challenges found in rural situations. However, the entirety of this experience is not unique to rural churches and many of the circumstances encountered would equally apply in the urban context.

The writing of this book has been prompted, to some degree, by the supposition that Sunday school happens each week on Sunday morning. The hope is that this book will encourage children's leaders in smaller churches to think outside the usual 'Sunday school' model so that they can find a way to work with more children more effectively. With a bit of lateral and creative thinking, perceived weaknesses can become strengths and the end result will be that children's work, even in a small church, can become vibrant and successful.

If your situation is urban, this book may still prove useful. You may feel that you need to start reaching children who are not coming to church on Sunday, and perhaps some of the ideas in this book will give you some pointers to how this might be achieved. Alternatively, perhaps numbers are falling and you need to look at ways to redress the situation.

GETTING STARTED

First of all, you will need to think carefully about your situation and how to work with or around any potential difficulties. Decisions about what you are going to do, where it will happen, when it will happen, and who is going to be involved are all vital.

When choosing a venue, there may be a number of options, such as a village hall or school hall. However, you are likely to need to hire these venues and you will probably be unable to keep your materials on the premises. As an alternative, you might like to consider using your church building. It is likely that the use of the building will be free, and you are more likely to be able to make arrangements to store materials *in situ*. Also, the richness of resources for Christian teaching and the subconscious osmosis of the wealth of symbols employed in a church are excellent.

However, the main problem with using the church building, particularly in a very old church, will be the lack of modern facilities. It is essential that the building can be heated sufficiently, particularly during the winter. You will also need light (natural or artificial) so that the children can see to do any craft activities. With regard to toilet facilities, if one of your group's leaders, or perhaps another member of the congregation, lives close enough, it may be possible to arrange for the children to use their facilities. You will need to draw up procedures for this, for child protection reasons (discussed later in this chapter).

Many old churches lack kitchen facilities, and you may need to arrange your planning accordingly. For example, it is likely to be impractical for the children to cook anything very elaborate, although simple things such as peppermint creams can work well. If a member of the congregation living nearby is prepared on occasion to allow you to use their oven, the children can even make biscuits or bread, which can be taken out of the building for baking and brought back later.

Deciding which day to hold workshop sessions, how often they should be held and how long they should go on for will depend on a number of local factors. With regard to frequency of sessions, it is best to be realistic about what you will be able to do. Running a two-hour workshop is very intensive while the session is in progress, and also consumes time and mental energy in terms of planning and preparation. Running this type of activity every week would certainly be very hard work. Conversely, smaller shorter sessions held fortnightly may lead to a dwindling in attendance. Therefore, it may be more effective to concentrate resources into monthly workshops. If people expect a bigger 'event' less often, they will make more effort to ensure that they can go: if they miss it, the next chance will be some time off.

The length of each session is also important. The model used in this book runs for two hours. If this is followed by a short act of worship, the time will be extended by up to half an hour. When deciding on this point, think about how the children will be arriving. If parents will be driving them—perhaps from other villages some miles away—it is a good idea to make sure the parents will have enough time to go and do something else, or to go back home and have more than a ten-minute cup of tea, before turning round and driving back to collect their children. In other words, the sessions need to be long enough to make it worthwhile for the parents as well.

PUBLICITY

Telling people about the sessions you propose to run is important. Sending out invitations is a very good way to make sure people know that the workshops are taking place. Even when the pattern is established, it is still good practice to send out invitations giving information about the next session. Make sure the sessions are advertised in your church magazine or newsletter and announced at services. Make sure that baptism families are told about the children's work, and receive invitations too. The most important publicity will be by word of mouth, so your workshops are likely to grow in popularity once they start. Children will tell their friends and their parents will tell their friends.

FUNDING

Children's work invariably needs financial support. You may find that there are trust funds available or your PCC or governing council may allow you a budget. Unless absolutely necessary, it is best not to charge admission for children to attend. It is essential that any child who wishes to come should be able to do so. In addition, it is not recommended that any collection should be taken at a concluding act of worship. If parents wish to make a donation, provision should be made for them to do so, but there should be no reference made to this possibility.

You may wish to raise funds for a named charity to which the children wish to give, but equally, a general fundraising effort, perhaps by the PCC, would be helpful if funds are required for the running of the club itself. Ideas for fundraising can be found on our website.

CHILD PROTECTION AND HEALTH AND SAFETY

It is essential that you give both child protection and health and safety considerable attention. Your diocese (or equivalent) should be able to provide you with detailed information about what is required and how to go about fulfilling the requirements. It is vitally important that all your helpers have Criminal Records Bureau clearance and that you comply with the law by making sure that you run your sessions with proper attention to child protection and health and safety. Remember that the safeguards are there to protect not only the children who are in your care but also the adult helpers. Where you need assistance, ask for help. Obtaining clearance and holding records can easily be done by someone who wishes to support your children's work but may not be able to offer any physical help.

Make sure you know how a child's disclosure of neglect or abuse at home should be handled. Check this with your diocese, or equivalent, too. You are likely to find that there is someone nominated by the diocese to deal with these issues, which will avoid the situation (particularly destructive in close-knit communities) of neighbours being told, or perhaps the vicar becoming aware of too much detail, which will make his or her continuing ministry to the family difficult. You may think that this scenario is unlikely in a small community where everyone appears to know everyone else's business, but we can never be sure what goes on behind closed doors. Waiting until after a disclosure has been made before finding out how it should have been handled is too late.

Check the requirements for the ratio of adults to children at your sessions. This will depend on the age of the children present, but in any case you should always have enough adults to ensure that there are at least two present at any time with any child. Allow for the possibility of one adult having to leave the room for some reason: there should always be two left behind. At least one adult in each session should be a qualified first aider. If you need more people to be qualified, find out about local training courses for child first aid.

REGISTRATION

Make sure you have documentation giving certain minimum information about the children in your care. A simple registration form will be sufficient for this. It should give the name and date of birth of the child, contact details including emergency contact details, information about any allergies and the name of the child's doctor. Permission for things like administration of first aid and taking of photographs could also be included. A draft example is provided on the website, www.barnabasinchurches.org.uk.

Also, you will need to register each child as they arrive so that you have an ongoing record of attendance. In this way, you will be able to keep track of those children who attend regularly and follow up those who have not attended for a period of time. As you register each child, write his or her name on a simple badge made from a self-adhesive label. You may get to the stage where you can preprint badges with the children's names (have blanks available for new attenders). You could shape the badges according to your theme or the name of your club or choose a simple fish shape as a sign that it is a Christian club.

A signing in and signing out form for parents as they drop and collect children will ensure that you know which children are present at any time. The form should also have space for a parent to notify you if someone else will be collecting their child. An example form is provided on the website, www.barnabasinchurches.org.uk.

HEALTH AND SAFETY

Check with your PCC or governing council that you have appropriate insurance cover. You should ensure that the electrical checks on wiring and equipment, and the fire extinguisher checks, are up to date. Make sure you know where the fire escape exits are, and that they are easily accessed in the event of fire. Doors may need to be watched, however, to ensure that children don't escape during the session.

Look at the building or room(s) you will be using, from a child's point of view. If you are using an old church, be aware of hard and possibly steep stone steps, unguarded heaters, things that are shouting out to be climbed, or other hazards. No room can ever be completely safe, but you must take every precaution to ensure the safety of the children in your care.

THEMED PROGRAMMES

INTRODUCTION

Before embarking on any of the themes in this book, there are a number of considerations that apply equally to all the programmes.

First of all, make sure that planning and preparation is thorough. To ensure that it is, it is a good idea to write everything down and make sure all the helpers have a copy. It is also helpful to try out all the craft ideas before you ask the children to do them. That way, you will find where any little difficulties lie, or if there is some particular adaptation you will need to make for the materials you have available. You will notice that different children take different amounts of time to do the same activity, so it is also a good idea to have available something to occupy children who finish an activity ahead of time. Ideas include a whiteboard or blackboard to doodle on, some construction toys or books.

Remember that children can get noisy and carried away by the excitement of the moment. Investing in a bell or other method of making an even louder noise to get their attention is very worthwhile and saves untold damage to the vocal chords.

PROGRAMMING AND PREPARATION

The programmes in this book can be expanded or contracted, depending on the number of children attending. For example, to expand a programme, the learning of a song could easily be inserted. Also, it makes sense to have smaller groups of children doing different activities at the same time. For example, if you have three activities running before a break, and there are twelve children in the group, you could divide them into three groups of four and run each activity three times concurrently, with the children circulating between activities. You do need extra helpers for this, but it is well worthwhile for the extra attention you can give to each child.

When considering the order of activities, bear in mind that if you want displays to be ready before the children leave, paint or glue will need time to dry. Work that the children are taking home will also be easier to carry if it isn't too wet. If they are baking, biscuits and bread need time to cook!

The number of different activities needed to keep children occupied and involved will vary greatly, depending partly on the age of the children. Most nine-year-olds can stick at an activity for longer than a four-year-old. The nine-year-old will be more meticulous and will get bored less quickly; so older children tend to need fewer activities to fill a two-hour session. That said, some activities, even for younger children, will engross them more than you might have anticipated, so you may find yourself running out of time. You will need to be flexible and have a strategy for cutting activities if, half-way through the session, it looks as if there will not be time for everything. Although this may mean wasted preparation, materials can always be used in future sessions, and it is better to have too much than to be floundering around trying to fill the last half-hour because you have too little.

Some of the activities suggested involve a certain amount of time in preparation. For a few (but not all, by any means), some more expensive materials might be required. If these are too expensive, there are plenty of other activities to choose from. Once you have got your sessions underway, you will find that spending a little extra money occasionally is worthwhile. You will also need to consider how to deal with the inevitable messiness resulting from craft activities. Tables may need to be covered with newspaper or, better still, plastic-covered fabric cut to size, which can simply be wiped clean after the session. You will need kitchen towel or wipes for some activities, and hand-washing equipment.

TELLING STORIES

As you will see, most of the activities are connected to a Bible story, or a theme for which you could have two or three stories. There are a number of low-tech but very effective ways to tell stories. If you are just going to read the story (and there is nothing wrong with that), it is a good idea to practise beforehand, or even try it out on another person. Make sure you understand the flow of the story so that you can read it well without getting caught out by unusual punctuation. If you are reading from the Bible, read a few versions and pick the one that the children will understand best. If there are pictures, use them and make sure the children can see them. Make sure you read clearly and slowly enough for everyone to hear and understand.

It is a good idea to get some variety into your storytelling, which will make it easier to keep the children's attention. Some suggestions are outlined below, all of which are achievable without too great an expense. The list is not exhaustive!

STORYTELLING USING 'GODLY PLAY'

The *Godly Play* method of telling Bible stories works fantastically well and is becoming more widespread. It is certainly worth finding a short training course on this technique and devoting some resources to buying or making the materials that are required. The methodology was developed in the United States by Jerome Berryman and is based on the Montessori educational model. Details of *Godly Play* resources are given in the Bibliography on page 189.

In this method of storytelling, the storyteller uses (in most instances) simple wooden figures placed on a fabric underlay, or in a box of sand if it is a desert story. In effect, this becomes a stage. The storyteller has no eye contact with the hearers, but instead concentrates on the figures themselves. The story is told in simple but specific language and uses slow, deliberate movements in the placing and moving of the figures and in the gestures of the storyteller. The effect of this is that the story itself and not the storyteller becomes the main focus of attention. The children are typically very calm and become almost entranced by the story, although adult helpers are needed to sit with them in order to deal with any cases of restlessness or interruptions and so allow the storyteller to maintain concentration.

PERFORMANCE STORYTELLING

At the other end of the spectrum, you might like simply to learn the Bible passage and recite it from heart instead of reading it. This way, the storyteller removes the book that can act as a barrier between teller and hearers, maintaining constant eye contact with the hearers and concentrating on putting life into the story. Hearing the Bible in this way can be enthralling. However, if you find it too difficult to learn the passage word for word, once you are familiar enough with it you could always retell the story in your own words instead.

You could also experiment with dramatic readings, requiring two or more people reading the story. *The Dramatised Bible* is an excellent resource if you don't wish to create your own scripts.

INTERACTIVE STORYTELLING

There are several techniques you can employ to make your storytelling interactive.

★ Consider using sound effects at appropriate parts of the story. For example, if there is a knocking at the door, arrange for someone at the back of the room to make a very loud (preferably cavernous) knocking sound at the appropriate moment. This type of effect works even better if you are telling the story from memory. However, don't overdo 'sit-up-and-take-notice' effects!

★ Using audience participation is also very effective. Ask the children to make a noise, or shout a word, or do an action whenever you say a particular word. Then work your way through the story with the children supplying the sound effects. You may need to edit the original text slightly to increase the frequency of the words to which they are responding.

★ If you're using a repetitive story, ask the children to say a response. For example, if you are telling the creation story, prepare a large smiling face drawn on a large circle of card and ask the children to say 'it is good' every time you hold it up.

★ Using objects can also be effective. In a small group, you could use feely boxes, so that the children have to guess what the items are. Use objects that are visible to everyone and either line them up as the story unfolds or give them to the children to hold while the story is in progress.

★ Tell a story accurately; then, after an interval when the children have done other things, tell it again, but make it full of mistakes and see how many the children can spot. Make some of the mistakes deliberately funny and some of them less easy to spot.

★ If you are able to be slightly more 'high-tech', show the children a short clip of a video, such as *The Miracle Maker*. This can be very effective, particularly if it's a rare treat for your group.

GENERAL ACTIVITIES

Some activities can be adapted to most themes. For example, singing, painting, drawing, modelling using junk, clay or play dough, cutting and sticking can all be used to illustrate a wide variety of ideas. You will find basic recipes in Appendix 2 on pages 175–178, and basic craft skills in Appendix 3 on pages 179–181.

CONCLUDING THE SESSION

Children's workshops work very well if they are concluded with an act of worship to which parents, carers and members of the wider congregation are invited and welcomed. The children's work can be on display, and it is a good idea to ensure that the children have prepared something that is useful for the act of worship, perhaps contributing phrases to a prayer, some artwork relevant to the story or a new song to teach everyone else. This brings the whole event to a very satisfactory conclusion for children and adults alike.

If you view the whole event, workshop and service together as an act of worship, it will help to make sure the material is relevant. In effect, during the workshop the children are having their equivalent of a sermon (though they won't think of it this way) and learning about the word of God. But they are learning by doing and having fun, mixed with a little bit of listening and looking, rather than the other way round.

Lastly, make sure you enjoy your sessions too. Your cheerfulness and enthusiasm will help the children to be cheerful and enthusiastic.

AN ACT OF WORSHIP
FOLLOWING A SESSION

CHILDREN'S WORSHIP

Below are some suggestions for a short act of worship, designed to conclude a themed programme session. If you regard the session itself as supplying the place of the Bible readings and sermon, then a short service is a good way to conclude the event. Make sure you invite the children's parents, carers and anyone else who would like to come. It is important that there is good support from the adult congregation for the act of worship, so that it is not seen as 'just' for children.

You can make the service more relevant to the session by using some of the things the children have been doing. If they have been learning a song, ask the children to teach it to the adults; if they have made candles, you could light the candles on the altar. If they have written some prayers or ideas for prayers, you could read them out or ask the children to do it. You could tell the story on which the workshop has been based in a different way at the service, to give a different perspective on it, or perhaps the children might have prepared a different presentation of the story.

It is also a good idea to introduce elements that are the same as or similar to those that happen in a main Sunday morning service, so that there will be something familiar in a main Sunday service if any of the families decide to come along to one. Sharing the peace is a good place to start. The children will enjoy shaking hands with everyone else. You might also consider using a form of creed, and a form of confession (though perhaps not using identical words to those used in a formal service). A song version of the Gloria would also be appropriate. Because the act of worship is quite short, there will not be time to include much liturgy, so you might wish to consider using different elements in different months to help the children to become familiar with the overall pattern of Sunday worship.

You may find that the adults attending this act of worship starts to outnumber the Sunday morning congregation. In this way, you will be reaching people who would not come to any other service, as it is not just children who find long services, couched in archaic language, difficult. You will therefore find yourself ministering to adults as well as children.

A typical act of worship after a themed programme sessions might include:

* ☆ Introduction
* ☆ Song (which may or may not be a Gloria song)
* ☆ Form of confession or a thanksgiving or a creed
* ☆ Story
* ☆ Prayer (including the Lord's Prayer)
* ☆ Song
* ☆ Sharing the peace (usual words)
* ☆ Song
* ☆ Grace and final blessing

This format is very flexible and can be adapted to suit your need. For example, the order might be rearranged so that a version of the Gloria is sung or the creed is said immediately after the story.

ADULT WORSHIP

Of course, children should be welcomed at any church service and there are ideas on our website to help children to participate. However, it would be good to make a particular provision for children on special occasions. For example, if you have run a Lent course for the children (see website for details), provision could be made for them to be involved in the service on Easter Day by singing a song, teaching a prayer with actions, performing a tableau to illustrate the Bible story, or by having some of their craft work on display. Involving the children will encourage their parents and carers to attend the service too.

If children have been taking part in a particular project, such as designing church kneelers, it's a good idea to hold a service to celebrate this, and (in this instance) to dedicate the kneelers. The children who produced the designs and the adults who helped in the making of them will all want to be present.

Theme 1

ADVENT

The theme of Advent should be explored separately from Christmas and, ideally, run in late November or early December.

STORIES FOR ADVENT

The parable of the ten girls in Matthew 25:1–13 is a story about being prepared and is therefore a good starting point for an Advent workshop. An old pair of gloves can be transformed into the ten girls in the story by sticking felt or card faces on to the fingers of each hand. On one hand the faces will be smiling (wise), but on the other hand they will be sad (foolish). Tell the story using the gloves as visual aids. It is also very effective if you prime someone else, placed at the back of the room, to make a loud knocking sound at the appropriate moment.

Other parables about the kingdom of heaven suitable for Advent include:

★ The story about the mustard seed (Matthew 13:31–32)
★ The story about the yeast (Matthew 13:33)
★ A hidden treasure (Matthew 13:44)
★ The valuable pearl (Matthew 13:45–46)

All these short parables are excellent, particularly for younger children. If you wish to tell the story using *Godly Play*, you will find scripts in the *Godly Play* resources books (see Bibliography on page 189 for details).

If you are using the story of the yeast, show the children some fresh yeast and get them to touch and smell it. Add some to lukewarm water with some sugar and stir. Show the children what has happened to the yeast after about 15 minutes—it should be frothy on top with lots of air bubbles—and explain how this helps bread to rise.

DISPLAYS FOR THE CHURCH

JESSE TREE

 Time duration: 30 minutes

You will need: some twiggy branches, sand or gravel, a large plant pot, gold spray paint (optional), circles of card (as many as there are children attending the session), a hole punch, gold thread, stories from the Old Testament.

'Plant' a twiggy branch in a pot of sand or gravel. Make sure the pot is large enough to keep it stable. If desired, paint the 'tree' with gold spray paint to make it look even more effective.

Cut as many card circles as there are children attending your session. Punch a hole in each circle and thread some gold thread through it.

Have available a list of stories from the Old Testament that you'd like illustrated, or let the children choose their own. Ask the children to illustrate one story each on their circle. Suggestions for a small group might be creation (sun, moon and stars); fall (apple); flood (rainbow); Ten Commandments (stone tablets); wandering in the desert (footprints); prophets (prophet figure); King David (lute or musical symbol); Solomon's temple (precious stones or metal). There should also be a circle depicting the incarnation (perhaps a star).

Each child can add his or her circle to the Jesse tree, with the incarnation picture hanging from the topmost branch. Explain to the children while they are doing this activity that the stories in the Old Testament all lead up to the moment of Jesus' birth, when God became a human being.

THE KINGDOM OF HEAVEN IS LIKE...

 Time duration: 10 minutes

You will need: art materials, a digital camera (optional)

Ask the children to paint pictures on the theme, 'The kingdom of heaven is like...'. Their work will make a good display for your church. They may want to take their pictures home; if so, take photographs of the artwork before it disappears, to give you something to put on a display board.

CRAFTS FOR ADVENT

CLAY LAMPS

 Time duration: 30 minutes

You will need: a picture of a first-century oil lamp, air-drying clay.

Show the children a picture of a lamp similar to the ones that would have been used in the story of the ten girls, and ask them to model their own out of air-drying clay.

CROWNS

 Time duration: 10 minutes

You will need: pre-cut crown shapes, made from thin card, for each child, glitter, sequins, holographic paper shapes, fake 'jewels' and so on, glue, clear adhesive tape or stapler to secure the two ends of the crown.

This is a good activity to use if you are telling the story of the valuable pearl. Provide pre-cut crown shapes and ask the children to decorate them with glitter, sequins, holographic paper shapes, fake 'jewels' and so on. While they are carrying out the activity, talk about the kingdom of God being very precious.

HEART CARDS

 Time duration: 10 minutes

You will need: card, either heart-shaped or A4 folded in quarters, for each child, colouring materials, coloured or shiny paper (optional), a heart-shaped hole punch (optional).

Give each child a heart-shaped card to decorate, or use heart-shaped punches so that they can cut out hearts and stick coloured or shiny paper behind the holes to make their own Advent cards.

TREASURE HUNT

This activity also fits well with the story of the valuable pearl or the hidden treasure. Either make sure the clues are not too hard for your youngest children or make sure they have enough help. A small prize at the end is probably necessary, but make sure there is also a card with a Christian message on it, too.

To design the treasure hunt, use whatever is in your church. For more ideas on involving children in fundraising, see our website, which contains suggestions for a sponsored treasure hunt.

MUSTARD AND CRESS

 Time duration: 10 minutes

You will need: shallow trays or plastic plates, kitchen towel, mustard and cress seeds, simple stencils (optional), water.

This will work well with the mustard seed parable, although the children will have to wait a little while for the results. Use shallow trays or plastic plates, line them with kitchen towel and make them damp. Sow the seeds thinly on top. To be extra imaginative, sow the seeds through a stencil (the simpler the shape, the better—such as a cross), so that the seeds will grow in that shape.

GAMES FOR ADVENT

DISTRACTION RACE

This is one game that works well in a church full of pews. Give one of the children a book or a video or DVD case and get them to balance it on their head while walking down a central path in your room. Meanwhile, the other children stand on either side of the path (in the pews if you have them); they are not permitted to touch the child who is making the journey, but they can say anything to distract them from what they are trying to do (for example, 'Your shoelace is undone' often works!). We are often distracted from what God wants us to do.

PAPER CLOTHES

Divide the children into two (or more) groups. Explain that one member of each group is going to a wedding and ask them to nominate that person. Provide each group with a newspaper and a roll of masking tape, then give them a limited amount of time (say, ten minutes) to make a wedding outfit using the newspaper and tape.

PRAYERS FOR ADVENT

STAR PRAYERS

 Time duration: 10 minutes

You will need: a large sheet of black paper, pre-cut star shapes (two or three for each child), pens or pencils, Blu-tack.

This idea is good for some quiet time, or it can be used during prayers in a church service. Have a large sheet of black paper and a number of star shapes pre-cut out of some holographic paper. If they wish, children can write or draw their prayers on the back of the stars, then come and stick them on to the black paper.

Theme 2

CHRISTMAS

It can be a challenge to organize workshops at this time of year, partly because of the children's expectation and partly because before Christmas adults are likely to be over-busy and children over-excited. With this in mind, it is worth delaying the Christmas workshop until after Christmas, when the season has turned into a dismal January and there is less competition from other events. Consequently, you should get good attendance by much less excitable children.

STORIES FOR CHRISTMAS

Tell the traditional Christmas story from Matthew and Luke (Matthew 1:18—2:14; Luke 1:26–38 and 2:1–21), either from a modern translation of the Bible, such as the CEV, or from a children's Bible.

If you have time, you could then invite the children to retell the story themselves, using a magnetic theatre especially designed for the nativity. These are inexpensive to buy and readily available in craft and toy shops or from the Internet. If you need extra characters, they can always be improvised by, for example, making a shepherd's headdress and attaching a sheep made from felt. Choose two or three children to operate the theatre and give others jobs such as lighting the stage using torches. Additional characters, such as angels, or props, such as a star, can be attached to a stick and held above the theatre by extra operators.

31

If you are using Epiphany as a separate theme, hold back this part of the story until the time comes. If you are running just a Christmas theme, take the story on into Epiphany and, if necessary, change your theatre characters from shepherds to wise men at the appropriate time. You will need to put someone in charge of 'wardrobe' to achieve a smooth changeover.

DISPLAYS FOR THE CHURCH

STAINED-GLASS WINDOW

 Time duration: 15 minutes

You will need: black mounting board, cellophane in a selection of colours, glue, scissors, strong thread for hanging.

Make a large stained-glass window for display in your church. Draw your design on to a large piece of black mounting board. If you want the picture to be viewed from both sides, use the first board to mark where to cut a second, so that they are mirror images and fit together when placed back to back.

Ask the children to fill in the design by sticking different coloured cellophane over the spaces to make the picture. Then stick on the second mounting board to make, in effect, a cellophane sandwich. This will look good from either side, so perhaps you could suspend it in your church underneath an arch.

An example of a stained-glass window is available to download from the website, www.barnabasinchurches.org.uk.

Time duration: 20 minutes

You will need: pre-cut card, glue, glitter, sequins and shiny paper, pre-made icosahedron(s), strong thread for hanging.

This is a lesson in geometry! Basically this is a 20-sided three-dimensional shape with pyramids radiating from the outside. It will take quite a lot of drawing, cutting and scoring, and the drawing and cutting need to be accurate.

The 20-sided shape is made up of triangles, as shown in the diagram below. The best way to create each triangle is by using a ruler and compass. Make sure you remember to add tabs so that the shapes can be glued together.

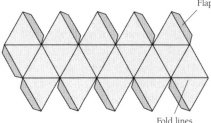

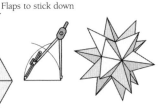

Flaps to stick down

Fold lines

This triangle is the same size as the base for the pyramid stellations

You will also need to prepare the points for the star. The basis of each point is a triangle the same size (or marginally smaller to ensure that everything fits together) as the triangles used for the 20-sided shape. The three triangles leading out from each shape in the icosahedron form the pyramid shape. Make them as long as you wish: the longer they are, the more 'pointy' the star will be.

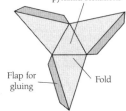

Flap for gluing

Fold

Making the stellations: this makes the spikes to stick on to the 20 sided-shape; you will need 20 of these

Make up as many icosahedrons as you need in advance. Prepare the card shapes you will need for the pyramid points: it's a good idea to score where the card will be folded. The children can decorate each shape with glitter, sequins and shiny paper (though not on the face that will be glued on to the icosahedron). The card shapes can then be glued up so that you have 20 individual very tall pyramids.

When the pyramids are ready, they can be attached to the icosahedron. Use glue that dries quickly and sticks well. Glue dots would work quite well, or a hot glue gun. The finished stars can be hung up as part of the Christmas decorations.

NATIVITY PLAYS

This is a time of year when we might feel obliged to mount a full-scale nativity play. Ironically, however, in a church context this is not always easy. It can be difficult to arrange a series of rehearsals at which you can guarantee that the children needed for even the leading roles will be present; getting children to learn lines outside of the school context is not easy; the burden of costume making is likely to fall on very few people and, after a round of school nativity plays, nativity play fatigue is likely to set in with both children and their parents. Here are some practical alternatives.

CARD FIGURES

 Time duration: 15 minutes

You will need: shapes of people and animals cut from heavy-duty cardboard boxes, white paper, paint for skin and features, brushes, fabric scraps, ribbon, felt, leather, wool and so on, glue, short garden canes or sticks, parcel tape, wire, tinsel.

Choose a text version of the nativity story and act it out using large-scale figures cut out of cardboard.

Use heavy-duty cardboard boxes to make the figures. Cut out the basic shapes using a sharp modelling knife. You will need as many figures (people and animals) as there are children. Make the figures large so that everyone in church will be able to see them.

Glue light-coloured or white paper to the hands and faces and get the children to paint them. They can then make the costumes for the figures from scraps of material, ribbons and felt. Some shops or market stalls will sell remnants very cheaply: if you mention that it is for your children's group, you may find that they are even more reasonable. For animals, use felt, wool and scraps of leather or fabric.

Attach the completed figures to short canes or sticks with parcel tape. Cover garden wire with tinsel to make haloes for the holy family.

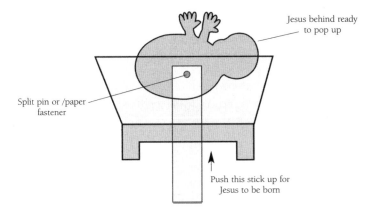

Jesus behind ready to pop up

Split pin or /paper fastener

Push this stick up for Jesus to be born

Create the figure of the baby Jesus in the manger using separate shapes for the manger and for the baby. The manger can then be held up on its own and, when the baby is born, the figure of the baby Jesus moved into place so that Jesus pops up in the manger.

Choose an adult or very competent child reader to be the

narrator and practise holding up the relevant figures as the story is told. Younger children will need an adult to give them their cue to hold up their figures at the appropriate time. The children don't need to learn any lines or move around, but they can still be proud to display their work and be part of a nativity story with a difference.

TABLEAUX

Get the children to form freeze-frame pictures as the nativity story unfolds. They will need to practise moving from one tableau to the next as quickly and smoothly as possible while a narrator reads the text.

Don't make the pictures follow too rapidly one upon the other. The congregation will need time to absorb each one and the children will need time to hold the pictures still. Don't try to do too many frames and don't be afraid of silence between one tableau and the next. Silence can be prolonged for longer than you might think.

There is no need for costumes, as the children can be dressed simply in plain sweatshirts and trousers.

SHADOW PLAY

 Time duration: 10 minutes

You will need: a large white sheet, a source of light.

The children make their shadow shapes by moving between the sheet and the light as the story unfolds. You will need to make sure the natural light levels are low enough for the shadows to show up. You will also need to experiment with the optimal distance between the sheet and the light and the way the shadows work from the audience side of the sheet. This may take a bit of time and patience.

SKETCHES

Read the nativity story to the children and then discuss with them how it might be turned into a short sketch or mime. Decide on the script and allocate simple lines to the children as appropriate. Alternatively, you could use a ready-written script or idea. You will need to practise your sketch before performing it to the congregation, but half an hour or so of practice should suffice and no costumes are needed.

CRAFTS FOR CHRISTMAS

STAR PICTURES

 Time duration: 15 minutes

You will need: pre-cut star shapes made out of shiny holographic paper, black paper or card (one sheet per child).

Make individual starry sky pictures to remind the children how Christ shines as a light in the darkness. Simply give each child some pre-cut star shapes for them to stick on to plain black paper or card.

SUN-SENSITIVE PAPER PICTURES

 Time duration: 15 minutes

You will need: sheets of sun-sensitive paper (one per child), flat items with a Christmassy theme, water for rinsing.

Sun-sensitive paper is available in kits at art and craft supply stores or on the Internet, and is a great way to make pictures.

Have available a selection of flat items, such as card stars, Christmas tree and angel shapes, or animal shapes such as donkeys, sheep and camels. (The selection can be varied for activities in other seasons too.)

Get the children to arrange the shapes on their sheet of sun-sensitive paper, and expose the paper to the light for the recommended time (this will vary depending on how much light there is). You will need to experiment in advance a few times to get it right.

Rinse the paper off and each child will have a home-made 'photograph'.

If the day is dull, or you are holding your event towards the end of the day, especially in the winter, the exposure time may be quite long. If light levels are too low, it may not work at all, so you may need to save this activity for a sunny day.

GLASS PAINTING

 Time duration: 15 minutes

You will need: a wide-necked jam jar for each child (big enough to put a tealight inside and light it) or a plain glass tealight holder, glass paints for outlining, glass paints for filling with colour, brushes.

Give every child either a wide-necked jam jar or a plain glass tealight holder. Give the children the glass paints and brushes and ask them to decorate their own lamps.

CRADLE CHRISTMAS TREE DECORATIONS

 Time duration: 10 minutes

You will need: wooden curtain rings, gold paint, cardboard egg boxes, scraps of gauze, small beads, glitter (optional), gold thread for hanging.

Before the session you will need to paint the curtain rings gold or silver and cut the egg boxes into segments, trimming them down a little so that they will sit comfortably in the curtain ring.

The children can then complete the cradles by decorating the ring and egg box cradle with glitter if desired.

Use the gauze to make baby-shaped bundles and glue a bead in place to represent Jesus' head. If you have a steady hand, you can draw closed eyes and features on the bead. Add the baby bundle to the egg box cradle and glue the cradle into the curtain ring. Using the gold thread, hang the curtain ring on the Christmas tree.

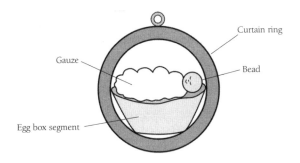

GAMES FOR CHRISTMAS

PASS THE PARCEL

 Time duration: 10 minutes

You will need: crêpe paper, an old Christmas card, cut up to make a jigsaw, a prize for the centre of the parcel, plus extra prizes for everyone to share, CD player and some Christmassy music.

This is a good time of year to play pass the parcel. Remind the children that at Christmas we are giving thanks for God's gifts to us, as well as giving each other presents.

Use crêpe paper to make the layers of wrapping paper. Cut up an old Christmas card to make a jigsaw and hide the pieces between the layers.

Sit the children in a circle and play some music as the parcel is passed around the circle, allowing a child to unwrap a layer in the traditional way when the music is stopped. As the parcel is unwrapped, get the children to put the picture together in the centre of the circle.

The last child to unwrap the parcel wins the prize at the centre, but also have available a prize that everyone can share to endorse the Christmas theme.

CHRISTMAS QUIZ

Older children enjoy quizzes. You will need to tailor your quiz to the children's biblical knowledge. It's a good idea to add some easier questions to the mix or, if you wish, some general questions about popular television programmes, current children's films or football.

The quiz may include the following questions.

★ What was the name of the angel who told Mary
   she would have a baby?   *Gabriel*
★ What was Mary's future husband called?   *Joseph*
★ Where did they live?   *Nazareth*
★ Why did Joseph have to go to Bethlehem?   *Census*
★ What was the name of the king at the time?   *Herod*
★ What was the name of the Roman emperor?   *Augustus*
★ Who were the first to be told that Jesus had
   been born?   *Shepherds*
★ Who told them?   *Angels*
★ What kind of room was Jesus born in?   *Stable*
★ Where did Mary put him to bed?   *Manger*
★ In which town did Jesus grow up?   *Nazareth*
★ Why do we give presents?   *Discuss!*
★ Who started the custom of Christmas trees?   *Prince Albert*
★ What are the four weeks before Christmas called?   *Advent*
★ What is the season after Christmas called?   *Epiphany*
★ What colour does the church use at Christmas?   *White*
★ In what other season does the church use this colour?   *Easter*

PRAYERS FOR CHRISTMAS

CANDLE PRAYERS

 Time duration: 10 minutes

You will need: tealight candles (at least one per child), silver
sand (obtainable from a toy shop), a long taper and matches.

Children always enjoy lighting candles. Place some tealight candles in a tray of sand. Have a brief discussion about the things the children would like to pray for. Light a long taper and invite the children to come and light a candle each (properly supervised) while they add a bit to the prayer.

Theme 3

CHRISTINGLE AND EPIPHANY

The Christingle service is often held before Christmas, but if Christingle is a tradition in your church, you may wish to consider holding the service after Christmas when things are less busy and linking it to a workshop on the theme of light. Alternatively, you may wish just to celebrate Epiphany; many of the activities in this session would suit either theme.

STORIES FOR CHRISTINGLE AND EPIPHANY

The story of Epiphany is the story of the wise men's journey to Bethlehem to find the baby Jesus. The story can be found in Matthew 2:1–12, but you may wish to recap the whole story of Christmas as an introduction to this particular part of the Christmas narrative. The theme of light also links to the opening chapter of John's Gospel (John 1:1–5) and to the beginning of the story of creation (Genesis 1:1–5).

If you are making Epiphany lanterns (see page 48), you can use them to tell the Epiphany story. Light as many tealight candles as you need before you start: this will depend on the figures you have chosen to decorate the lanterns. Line up the lanterns between you and the candles.

As you get to the part in the story where the character or object appears, carefully put the relevant lantern over the candle, so that the silhouette faces the children. Make sure the children keep a good distance from the candles so that everyone can see and no one gets hurt.

A GIANT CHRISTINGLE

NB: Before you make your giant Christingle, check that the finished item will go through the doors from its place of manufacture to wherever it will be used!

 Time duration: 30 minutes (pre-session preparation)

You will need: giant-sized balloon (about 1 metre diameter) from a party shop, greetings card shop or the Internet, vaseline, newspaper, wallpaper paste (without fungicide), piece of plastic drainpipe about 1.2 metres in length, bucket filled with dry sand or gravel, small plastic flowerpot, large candle, four robust cardboard tubes, such as wrapping paper inner rolls, orange tissue paper, a wide red ribbon at least 2 metres in length (depending on the size of balloon), bubble wrap, shiny paper, paper clips, red crêpe paper.

A giant home-made Christingle has quite a 'wow' factor. Before the session, blow up the giant balloon and cover it with a layer of Vaseline (you will need some help with this).

Tear up the newspaper and glue it to the balloon in layers. Continue layering the papier mâché until there is a thick and even coating. (You will probably need more layers than you think.) Leave a circular gap of approximately 10 cm around the neck of the balloon.

Use orange tissue paper for the final layer. (Don't worry if the newsprint shows through, as this makes an effective representation of the world.)

While the papier mâché is drying, take care to keep the temperature constant. The air inside the balloon will expand and contract according to the outside temperature and this could cause the papier mâché to split or collapse if the temperature is variable.

Once the shell has hardened, the balloon can be deflated and removed. Push the piece of plastic pipe (available from plumbers' merchants) through the bottom of the sphere. Cut a hole in the top of the sphere to allow the pipe to just poke through the top.

Place the long end of the pipe in the bucket of dry sand or gravel (if it is damp the papier mâché will go soggy) so that the 'orange' stands upright. The bottom of the 'orange' should rest on the top of the bucket.

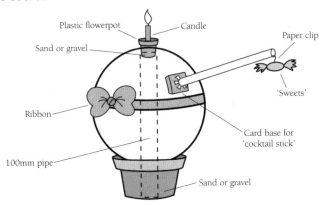

At the top of the sphere, insert the flowerpot into the pipe so that it sits comfortably inside the pipe. Fill the flowerpot with dry sand or gravel and plant a large candle inside it.

Use the cardboard tubes to make the four sticks. Attach them by making a 'plate' to which the tubes can be fixed so that they stand upright, before gluing to the 'orange' (see diagram). You will need to touch up the orange colour round these plates with a final layer of orange tissue paper.

Glue the red ribbon around the centre of the 'orange', slightly above the 'equator' (to prevent the ribbon falling off) and tie in a bow.

Form the bubble wrap into bundles to represent sweets and cover with shiny paper. Straighten out the paper clips and use them to secure the 'sweets' to the four tubes.

Cover the bucket with crêpe paper.

You can then use the giant Christingle as part of your prayer activity with the children (see p. 56).

CRAFTS FOR CHRISTINGLE AND EPIPHANY

CHRISTINGLE BANNERS

 Time duration: 30 minutes

You will need: two large rectangles of hessian or heavy-weight upholstery or curtain fabric, measuring approximately 0.5 metre long by 1 metre wide, machine hemmed along one of the shorter sides to form a casing through which the broom handles or poles can be threaded, two broom handles or similar, thick twine or curtain cord, fabric paints, sequins, beads, scraps of fabric and felt, lengths of red ribbon, scraps of thin cord in a selection of colours, glue.

Use the symbolism of the Christingle to discuss with the children how the different items represent the gifts that God gives us, both spiritual and physical.

Lay the rectangles of fabric out and explain that one banner will represent the incarnation and the other redemption. The central symbol for incarnation is the candle, which represents the light coming into the world. The central symbol for redemption is a cross, which can be formed from the red ribbon, to represent Jesus' death on the cross.

Using these two symbols as the main theme for the respective banners, invite the children to decorate each one. Have available a selection of fabric paints, scraps of fabric, sequins and beads. Glue each item to the banner and leave it to dry.

When the banners are dry, thread a pole through the top of each one and use thick twine or curtain cord to hang. The banners may be displayed in the church.

There is an example of a Christingle banner on the website: www.barnabasinchurches.org.uk.

CHRISTINGLE COLLAGES

 Time duration: 20 minutes

You will need: a sheet of heavy-weight A1 card or a prepared collage board, colouring materials or paints, sequins, beads, scraps of fabric, scraps of shiny paper, scraps of thin cord in a selection of colours, magazines, glue.

This activity is similar to the Christingle banners, but uses collage materials instead of fabrics and is suitable for younger children. The finished collage will show the world, representations of the seasons and pictures of the fruits of the seasons. Use pictures of branches or real branches to demonstrate the seasons, with pictures the children have drawn or pictures cut from magazines to demonstrate the fruits of the seasons.

Begin the activity by discussing with the children how the Christingle orange represents the world and the sticks represent the gifts that God gives us throughout the year.

Lay the card out and explain that the collage will represent the world, the seasons and the fruits of the seasons. It may help the children to have an outline sketched on to the card, so that they can envisage the completed picture before they start.

Have available a selection of colouring materials or paints, scraps of shiny paper and fabric, sequins and beads. Invite the children to decorate the card by gluing items to form the collage. Leave to dry.

When the collage is dry it may be displayed in the church.

EPIPHANY LANTERNS

 Time duration: 15 minutes

You will need: large plastic lemonade bottles, white poster paint and ordinary flour (or acrylic paint), sheets of white paper, tealight candles, matches, an ice-cream container of dry sand or a bucket of water.

First of all, remove the labels from the bottles. Cut the top and base off each bottle so that you have a number of clear plastic tubes. Paint the inside of each tube, using either poster paint thinned a little and mixed with flour to help it stick to the plastic or acrylic paint, so that the tubes are still translucent. The paint mustn't be too thick.

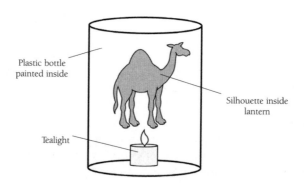

Cut the following shapes from the white paper: a star, the three wise men, a camel, baby Jesus, Mary and Joseph. Templates for the shapes can be found on pages 182–185. Glue the shapes on to the inside of the plastic tubes (one per tube).

Light the tealight candles and place a tube over each candle so that the light shines through the 'lanterns' but the silhouette of the figure is clear. Tell the Epiphany story using these lanterns.

NB: The lanterns are not fireproof and should be handled with care by responsible adults. Sand or water should be kept close by in case a candle catches the paper silhouette alight. If the children take the lanterns home, they and their parents should be issued with a warning about fire hazards.

EPIPHANY PICTURES

 Time duration: 15 minutes

You will need: household candles, a bowl of hot (not boiling) water, sheets of coloured paper, watery black paint or ink, paintbrushes.

This activity is designed to reveal what can't be seen. Give the children a sheet of coloured paper each and invite them to do a drawing using ordinary household wax candles. Warm the candles first in some hot water so that they are softened (although the children will still need to press quite hard to make their pictures).

When they have completed their drawings, point out that it's hard to see what they have drawn. Then let them paint some weak black paint or ink over the picture so that the picture is revealed. (You will need to experiment to determine optimum dilution of the paint.)

While the children are drawing, talk to them about how Jesus was revealed to us and explain that Epiphany means 'showing'.

CROWNS

 Time duration: 10 minutes

You will need: strips of medium-weight card, with spikes cut on one side to create a crown shape, pasta shapes, silver or gold paint, gummed paper shapes, glitter or glitter glue, sequins, clear adhesive tape.

Give each child a card crown shape. Let the children decorate their crown using fake 'jewels' made from gold and silver painted pasta shapes, and other collage materials. This activity can also be used for other occasions.

TAPESTRY PICTURES

 Time duration: 15 minutes

You will need: large-gauge canvas cut into pieces measuring approximately 15cm x 20cm, pen to mark the design on to the canvas, tapestry wool, tapestry needles, large beads in a selection of colours, scissors.

Children really enjoy doing tapestry work. When working the canvas, it's best to use long stitch, particularly with younger children, as this covers the canvas quickly and gives almost instant results. Christingle designs have been used here, but other designs could be used at other times of the year.

It's a good idea to make up 'kits' in advance. The design needs to be easy to reproduce so that it can be copied on to the canvas as many times as you need. Work one picture beforehand in order to calculate how much wool of each colour is required, then cut the wool into equal lengths and count how many lengths are needed for the design.

Use beads to represent the seasons of the year (check that the holes through the centre of the beads are large enough for the eye of the tapestry needle to pass through). Children can take any unfinished work to complete at home.

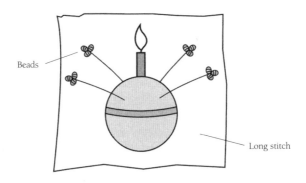

STAINED-GLASS WINDOW PICTURES

 Time duration: 15 minutes

You will need: A5 sheets of black card (two per child), coloured tissue paper or coloured cellophane, glue.

Place two sheets of card together and cut out shapes through both pieces to create a stencil effect. You could use a candle shape or a more adventurous design.

On one piece of card, glue coloured tissue paper or, for greater effect, coloured cellophane over the design to create a stained-glass window. Glue the second piece of card over the first to sandwich the tissue or cellophane. Take care to ensure that the design lines up on both sheets of card.

The pictures can be fixed in a real window to be displayed at full effect.

If you wish, this activity could form the display for your church, rather than the children taking them home.

ILLUMINATED MANUSCRIPTS

 Time duration: 15 minutes

You will need: printed copies of the Bible verse (see below), shiny pens and crayons.

This activity is good for any 'light'-themed programme and could also be used for a Bible Sunday workshop.

Show the children some pictures of illustrated manuscripts—how beautifully and intricately they were designed—and ask them to produce their own. (You can find samples in your local library or on the Internet.)

Give each child the printed text of a suitable Bible verse, such as John 1:5: 'The light keeps shining in the dark, and darkness has never put it out'. Type the text using an attractive computer font, enlarged so that it fills a page. Print out on to sheets of plain paper.

Provide shiny pens and crayons for the children to use to create their design around the text. For older children, omit the first letter of the first word (in this case the letter 'T') so that they can create an illuminated letter at the beginning of the verse.

BEESWAX CANDLES

Buy sheets of beeswax in different colours, and lengths of candle wick. Make the candles by laying the wick along the wide edge of the beeswax sheet and rolling it up with the wick inside. The sheets can be cut into different shapes for different effects and more than one colour used, if desired.

For a multicoloured effect, cut rectangular sheets in half to make triangles. Let the children choose two triangles of contrasting colours. Trim about 2cm from the long edge of one of the triangles. Put them together, with the smaller triangle underneath.

Press the wick into the beeswax along the second longest edge and roll up carefully. Younger children will need some help to get the roll started off. You should end up with a stripy candle.

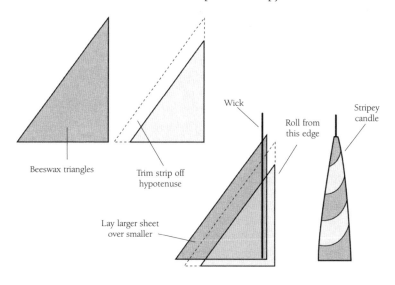

Beeswax triangles

Trim strip off hypotenuse

Lay larger sheet over smaller

Wick

Roll from this edge

Stripey candle

CANDLE NO-BAKE CHOCOLATE CAKE

A no-bake chocolate biscuit cake can be made even without a kitchen, although you will need to use a microwave or other suitable equipment in order to melt the chocolate.

Time duration: 20 minutes

You will need:
- ★ 600g chocolate
- ★ 250g butter or hard margarine
- ★ 100g rice cereal
- ★ 200g dried fruit
- ★ 200g digestive biscuits
- ★ Coloured sugar-coated chocolate beans (such as Smarties)

Line a baking tray with baking parchment. Put 400g of the chocolate in a bowl with the butter and melt together (use a microwave or, taking extra care, place the bowl over a saucepan of simmering water).

Put the biscuits in a strong polythene food bag and crush them with a rolling pin. Make sure they are not reduced to powder: there should be some reasonable lumps left. Add the crushed biscuits, rice cereal and dried fruit to the melted chocolate mixture.

Put the mixture into the baking tray, smooth it out and press it down well with an implement such as a wooden spoon or potato masher.

To prepare the topping, melt the remaining 200g of chocolate and spread it over the cake. Let the chocolate topping solidify slightly. Use the 'cool' coloured chocolate beans (the greens, blues and mauves) to make a candle shape, mosaic style, on the cake. The 'hot' colours (reds, oranges and yellows) can be used to make the flame shape on top.

RECIPE ADAPTED FROM *SEASONS AND SAINTS FOR THE CHRISTIAN YEAR*
BY NICOLA AND STUART CURRIE (NATIONAL SOCIETY/CHP, 1998)

This activity can be adapted for other occasions, just by changing the shape of the decoration on top. For example, you could make red and yellow flames for Pentecost, or the words 'happy birthday'.

GAMES FOR CHRISTINGLE AND EPIPHANY

CHRISTMAS QUIZ

Set a quiz using some of the suggested questions below. You might also include some easier questions, as well as general questions about popular television programmes, current children's films or football.

* ☆ How did the wise men find Jesus?
  Star
* ☆ How many wise men were there?
  We don't know, but as there are three gifts mentioned, we always presume that there were three wise men
* ☆ Where did the wise men look for Jesus first?
  Herod's palace
* ☆ They brought gold and… what were the other two gifts?
  Frankincense and myrrh
* ☆ What did Herod order when the wise men didn't return?
  Kill all children two years and under
* ☆ How did Mary and Joseph know they had to escape?
  Angel warned them
* ☆ What is the main fruit used in a Christingle?
  Orange
* ☆ What does it represent?
  The world
* ☆ What are the other components?
  Candle, ribbon, sticks, sweets
* ☆ What do they represent?
  Jesus' birth and death, seasons, gifts
* ☆ Which organization benefits from Christingle services?
  The Children's Society

THANK YOU PRAYERS

Have a discussion about what we are thanking God for as part of the Christingle celebrations. Make the ideas into a prayer, perhaps using a simple response like 'Thank you, Lord'.

If you have made a giant Christingle, talk about the symbolism of each item and say a short prayer over them. The items represent:

* ☆ Orange: the world
* ☆ Ribbon: Christ's suffering (and God's love)
* ☆ Sticks: the four seasons
* ☆ Sweets: fruits of the seasons
* ☆ Candle: Christ, the light of the world

Theme 4

LENT

The beginning of Lent is traditionally marked with pancakes on Shrove Tuesday before the time of preparation for Easter begins on Ash Wednesday. The six weeks of Lent are quite a solemn period in the Christian year, but there are some creative ways to mark the season with children.

STORIES FOR LENT

The story of Jesus' temptation in the wilderness is a key story for Lent. The story can be found in Matthew 4:1–11, Mark 1:12–13 and Luke 4:1–13. The account can be told in a variety of ways, including using the three-dimensional approach of *Godly Play* (see page 189 for resources). Another useful resource for Lent is the book *Living in a Fragile World* by Peter Privett, published by BRF. This book focuses on the issues of conservation and creation as a Lenten theme and is suitable for children from the age of seven. Alternatively, the film *The Miracle Maker* provides useful clips of the story of the life of Jesus.

TRANSITORY ART

Transitory art is art that is not stuck down or fixed, so it can be packed away when you've finished looking at it and the materials reused. It is very economic once you have acquired the initial items. There are no hard and fast rules for what can be used, but natural materials work well. Here are some suggestions.

☆ The church building is bare in Lent, as no flowers are taken into church during this period. However, displays to illustrate the seriousness of the season can be created using materials such as coir (coconut husk fibre), pine cones, driftwood, cork, wooden beads, feathers, shells, sand and scrunched-up tissue paper   .
☆ A desert display could be created using sand, small stones, driftwood; a toy snake (to represent the temptations by the devil), a scroll (to represent the scriptures), a model of a church (to represent the temple) and items to represent the kingdoms of the world (discuss with the children what these might be).

TEMPTATIONS FRIEZE

 Time duration: 20 minutes

You will need: a roll of lining wallpaper (unpasted), thin card, black backing paper and card, art materials, silver sand, scissors, PVA glue.

To go with your transitory art, you could make a three-part frieze to illustrate the three temptations of Jesus. You will need to divide the children into three groups, each group working on one frieze.

In the first group, cut some stones and loaves of bread (or slices of bread, which may be easier to depict) out of card and paint them to illustrate the temptation to change stones into bread. Spread a layer of PVA glue on the frieze and sprinkle some silver sand over it, then arrange the stones and loaves on and around the sand.

Meanwhile, the second group can create a night-time cityscape to illustrate the temptation of kingship over all the world. Splash a little white paint over black backing paper to make a starry night sky. Then, using black card (preferable a slightly different colour black), the children can make building shapes to stick on. Illuminated windows and neon signs can be made with chalks and pastels.

To illustrate Jesus' temptation to throw himself off the temple, so that everyone would see and follow him, the third group might make a frieze of lots of faces.

If you make separate friezes for each temptation you could display them on different walls in the church.

CRAFTS FOR LENT

LENTEN TREES

 Time duration: 10–20 minutes

You will need: sheets of white A4 paper, sheets of green A4 paper, colouring materials, pencils, scissors.

This activity emphasizes that Lent isn't just about giving up things (which is rather a negative view), but can also be about positive things such as giving some time to God or making time to help someone else.

Draw a simple tree trunk outline and branch shapes on a sheet of A4 paper and photocopy it on to white paper, so that each child has a sheet. Then draw five leaf shapes on a sheet of A4 paper and photocopy it on to green paper, again so that each child has a sheet.

If it is a dry day, the children could take their tree trunk paper outside and do bark rubbing on to the tree trunk shape. If not, pens and crayons can be used indoors.

When they have coloured their tree trunks, get the children to cut out the leaf shapes. On each leaf they should write or draw something to indicate a kind and helpful action that they could do for Lent. As each week of Lent passes, the children can stick the next leaf on to their tree. This works in a similar way to an Advent calendar.

If your children's group meets frequently enough, you might consider making a large Lenten tree for the whole group to use, with good deeds that have been agreed by the whole group.

PICTURE IN A BOX

 Time duration: 25 minutes

You will need: shallow boxes, such as those in which cheese triangles are sold, sheets of acetate, painting materials, corks, cut into thin slices, medium-weight pieces of card in a selection of colours, coloured cellophane, kitchen foil, tissue paper in a selection of colours, scraps of patterned paper, glue, scissors.

Cut a large hole in the lid to correspond with the shape of the box. (For example, if you are using cheese triangle boxes, the hole will be round.) Stick some acetate into the lid from the inside to form a window. Paint the lid frames to give a good finish. You will need one box per child.

Ask the children to think of the best possible place in the world—it could be a city or island or mountain or countryside—and ask them to make it into a three-dimensional picture in the box, using the materials supplied. They will need to start with the background, which can be stuck on to the base of the box. Layers can then be built up in front of the background, using the thin slices of cork to separate each layer of the design.

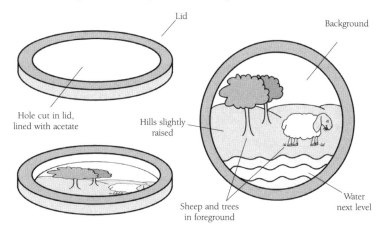

Lid

Background

Hole cut in lid, lined with acetate

Hills slightly raised

Water next level

Sheep and trees in foreground

STONE PAINTING

 Time duration: 15 minutes

You will need: large stones (from a garden centre or builders' merchant), painting materials, brushes.

Painting stones is always popular. During Lent this activity links well to Jesus' first temptation in the desert.

Give each child a stone. (If the stones are dusty, rinse them off and allow them to dry before they are painted.) With younger children, discuss the sort of theme they could paint on the stone to link in with the story of Jesus' temptations. Very young children could simply paint a cross. With older children, discuss things that are a temptation to them.

SAND PICTURES

 Time duration: 15 minutes

You will need: sand in different colours (from an aquatic supplier or craft shop), A4 sheets of medium-weight card (one per child), string, PVA glue, sheets of newspaper.

Give each child a sheet of card and get them to apply glue to it. Stick string on to the glued card to create a pattern and to separate the different colours of sand.

Sprinkle the picture with sand, shaking any excess sand off the card over a sheet of newspaper so that it can be collected up and reused. The children can let their imaginations run wild and design whatever they wish.

GAMES FOR LENT

STEPPING STONES

 Time duration: 20 minutes

You will need: kneelers, cushions, small mats or magazines, bowls of sweets.

Lay some kneelers, cushions, mats or magazines on the floor to make a stepping-stone pathway. (If using magazines, make sure they won't slip.) The distance between the stones will depend on the age and agility of the children. Place some tempting sweets in dishes, some within reach and others just out of reach.

As the children go down the path, tell them that they can have one sweet from any bowl they can reach, but they mustn't step or fall off the stepping stones.

DIRECTIONS GAME

 Time duration: 15 minutes

You will need: a large piece of sheeting (optional), fabric marker pen (optional).

If you wish, start by preparing a large compass, using a piece of sheeting cut into a circle, with the points of the compass marked out on it. Lay the 'compass' on the floor to help younger children remember which way is which.

Divide the children into pairs, and give one child in each pair a destination to which they must guide the other (to avoid overcrowding, make the destinations different for each pair).

Tell the children where the points of the compass are (in a church building, this is likely to be easy) and ask the child with the destination to give directions to the other child, using numbers of paces and points of the compass to get them there. The pairs can then swap so that everyone has a go.

When the children have completed this activity, talk to them about how we can use the Bible to give us directions and show us the right way to go. Make sure the children notice that the points of the compass form a cross.

A similar game is sometimes played by blindfolding the children. If your hall or meeting room is suitable for this, you can play by using left/right instructions instead of compass points. However, if you are using an old church building, there are likely to be too many changes in level and hard stone surfaces for this to be safe.

SIMON SAYS

Even younger children can enjoy this game as it is non-competitive. It links with the idea of doing what God says, as opposed to doing wrong. It is also incredibly effective in getting the children to sit down quietly and listen.

PRAYERS FOR LENT

SORRY PRAYERS

As Lent is an appropriate time for confessions, try introducing a children's version of the confession. For example, you might use one with actions—saying sorry for the wrong things we have seen (touch eyes) or heard (touch ears) or said (touch mouths) and so on. Don't forget to finish the prayer with an assurance of God's forgiveness.

Theme Five

MOTHERING SUNDAY

Mothering Sunday is a popular festival and families will often come to church to celebrate the day, even if they are not regular church-goers. When running the workshop, be sensitive to the reality that not all families consist of a mother, father and children. It is better to make people who 'do mothering' the focus of the theme, rather than just mothers. This way, fathers, carers, other relatives, teachers, childminders and nurses can also be included.

STORIES FOR MOTHERING SUNDAY

Read the story of Jesus in the temple as a boy (Luke 2:41–52), using a contemporary version of the Bible, or children's Bible. Alternatively, there are a number of stories about various biblical mums, such as the story of baby Moses, Hannah and baby Samuel, Elizabeth and baby John, and Mary and baby Jesus. Talk about the importance of their role as carers as well as mothers.

Follow this with a discussion about how Mothering Sunday is not just about mothers, but about everyone who 'mothers' us. Talk about what mothers do. You could write the children's responses on a flip chart, then talk about who apart from our mothers give us these things. You should get answers that include other members of the family, childminders, teachers in school, nurses and doctors at the hospital and so on. Then widen the discussion to talk about 'mother earth' and how she looks after us—all the essential things she provides that we need to survive (food, air, water, fuel and so on).

Then turn the conversation to 'mother church' and how she provides essential spiritual 'mothering' to keep us nourished in that way (baptism, teaching the Bible, fellowship, getting to know God and so on).

You might also talk about how time-consuming it is to look after something—to 'mother' it. Perhaps you could bring in a pet, preferably something furry, for the children to meet and then talk about how much love and care it needs. How much more do we need? You will need to ensure that none of the children have allergies to animals before doing this.

DISPLAYS FOR THE CHURCH

MOTHERING COLLAGE

 Time duration: 25 minutes

You will need: heavyweight A2 card or a prepared collage board, collage materials (coloured, patterned and shiny paper, card and so on), magazines, drawing materials (pencils, felt-tipped pens, paper), scissors, glue.

Prepare a collage board and divide it into three sections. In the first section draw the outline of a person, to represent mothers and other people who look after us. In the second section draw a circle to represent mother earth, and in the final one draw the outline of either a church or a cross to represent mother church.

Use collage techniques to fill in the shapes. You might use pictures the children have drawn themselves (on small pieces of paper) or pictures cut from magazines illustrating the type of mothering we receive from mothers, mother earth and mother church. Alternatively, children might prefer to fill in the shapes to look like a mother, the earth and the church respectively, using coloured paper or card. Label the shapes appropriately, so that it is clear what is being depicted.

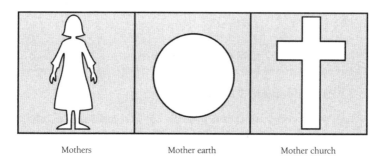

| Mothers | Mother earth | Mother church |

CRAFTS FOR MOTHERING SUNDAY

DAFFODIL CARDS

 Time duration: 15 minutes

You will need: yellow card or paper, bright green card or paper, card egg boxes, orange paint, A4 medium-weight card in pastel shades, pencils and felt-tipped pens, PVA glue and glue spreaders.

Have ready some yellow petals cut from yellow card or paper, and also some long leaves and stalks cut from bright green paper or card. Cut the egg boxes up into separate cups. If time is short, paint the egg box cups orange before the session. If you wish the children to do their own painting, you will need to allow time for the paint to dry.

If the children are doing their own painting, let them do this first.

Give each child a piece of pastel-coloured A4 card, folded in half widthways to make an A5-sized card. Get the children to write their messages inside the cards. The children need to stick a green stalk and pair of leaves on to the front of the card, with five yellow petals at the top of the stalk. Where the petals meet in the centre, stick the orange-painted segment of egg box to make the daffodil 'trumpet'.

FLOWER ARRANGING

 Time duration: 15 minutes

You will need: a selection of fresh cut flowers, small plastic containers, such as those used for shop-bought desserts (one per child), oasis, water, scissors

Share the flowers among the children, making sure that they have equal quantities and quality of sprays. Cut the oasis to fit inside each container. Soak the oasis. Allow the children to arrange the flowers by pushing the stems into the oasis, cutting the stems to size as appropriate.

The children can take these arrangements home for their mothers or carers. If there is time at the end of the session and flowers to spare, perhaps the children could make some arrangements for mother church, too.

BISCUIT BOXES

 Time duration: 20 minutes

You will need: squares of medium-weight card in a variety of colours, pencils, rulers, scissors, glue, stapler, glitter pens.

Pre-cut box shapes from light card, using the figure below as a guide. Make sure the boxes will be big enough to hold the biscuits (see cooking activity on page 71).

Fold the square in half diagonally both ways first. Next, fold each side in so that the edge meets the centre. You will now be able to see where the sides of the box are. If there is time, get the children to decorate the box with glittery pens. When this is done, you will need to pull the sides of the box up. The initial diagonal folds should make it easier to fold the excess flaps to the inside. These can either be glued or stapled to form the boxes.

If you wish, have some strips of paper or card ready to make a handle, which can be stapled on.

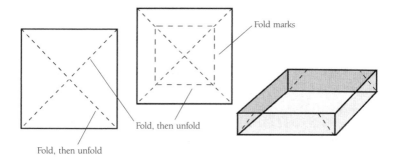

Fold marks

Fold, then unfold

Fold, then unfold

HENS AND CHICKS (TWO ACTIVITIES)

 Time duration: 15 minutes each activity (in 2 groups)

You will need: pom-poms (from craft suppliers), wool (optional), medium-weight card in white and orange, small beads, card egg boxes, crêpe or tissue paper in yellow and white, black felt-tipped pens (optional), collage materials (including feathers and fabrics), PVA glue, pencils, felt-tipped pens and colouring materials, scissors, stapler or clear sticky tape.

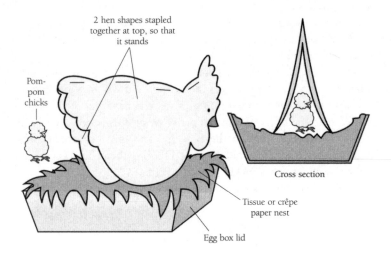

2 hen shapes stapled together at top, so that it stands

Pom-pom chicks

Cross section

Tissue or crêpe paper nest

Egg box lid

Either buy pom-poms or make your own. Cut hen shapes from the white card (two per child) using the template on page 186.

For the chicks, give each child two small beads for the eyes, and pieces of stiff orange card cut to shape for beaks and feet (see template on page 186).

Give each child the lid of an egg box to make a nest, and crêpe or tissue paper cut into thin strips for straw. Decide how many chicks each child will make and then give them a body pom-pom and a head pom-pom for each chick.

Children will need to glue a head pom-pom to a body pom-pom for each chick, then glue on the eyes, beak and feet. If the bead eyes are too fiddly for small children, either help them with these or use a black felt-tipped pen to mark the eyes on the pom-pom.

Fill the egg box lid with the shredded crêpe or tissue paper to make the nest.

For the mother hen, give each child two hen shapes. Make sure they understand which sides to decorate (the decorated sides should sit back-to-back as mirror images). Let the children decorate their hen shapes either with collage (feathers or fabric strips would look good) or with paint or pens.

When the hens are finished, attach the two parts together by stapling or taping the head and along the back. Next, pull the two pieces of card at the lower part of the hen apart so that the hen stands up and, in cross-section, makes a triangular shape with the nest. If necessary, make two gusset pieces out of card to keep this triangular shape in place, so that the chicks can fit underneath.

Making chicks and the hen will take some time, so you might prefer to use this as two activities, with children at one table making chicks and children at another making the mother hens.

COOKING FOR MOTHERING SUNDAY

GINGERBREAD MUMS

 Time duration: 15–25 minutes

You will need: gingerbread or biscuit dough (see recipe on page 176), shaped biscuit cutters (people, circles and crosses), greaseproof paper or baking parchment, clingfilm (to cover the finished biscuits or the dough if the children are taking their biscuits home unbaked), pens, baking sheets, hand-washing facilities.

Have ready a quantity of gingerbread or biscuit dough, or, if time allows, let the children help to make it. Roll the dough out on sheets of greaseproof paper.

Provide the children with shaped cutters. Use gingerbread ladies for mothering, plain circles for mother earth and crosses for mother church.

Place each child's biscuits on a square of baking parchment marked with the child's name, put them on a baking sheet and bake them either on the spot or, if you have no kitchen facilities, at a friendly neighbour's house. If neither of these options is possible, the children could take them home unbaked with instructions on how to bake them at home.

As with any food activity, check whether any child has allergies. If the biscuit dough you are using has egg in it, make sure the children don't eat the raw dough. You will need hand-washing facilities for before and after this activity: if you have no running water, a plastic washing-up bowl, water warmed in a kettle, some soap and towels will do just as well.

PRAYERS FOR MOTHERING SUNDAY

MOTHERING PRAYERS

 Time duration: 10–15 minutes

You will need: lightweight card, biscuit cutters used in the cooking activity above.

Use shapes cut from stiff paper of a person (you could draw round a gingerbread lady cutter), a circle and a cross to help with the prayers. Ask the children to write their prayers on these shapes. These can then be offered in whatever way seems fit—perhaps by attaching them to a board or display, or by collecting them in a plate and placing them on the altar, or you may wish to read them out. If you do intend to read them aloud, let the children know in advance that you will be doing this.

Theme 6

EASTER

Good Friday is an excellent day for holding a children's workshop, because it gives an opportunity to tell the children the whole story of Easter rather than missing out the bit between Palm Sunday and Easter Day, which often is the case if children only come to church on a Sunday.

STORIES FOR EASTER

The Easter story is a long one and needs to be presented in such a way as to hold the children's attention. One way to do this is by using objects to keep the children interested as the story unfolds. The outline for storytelling this way is given below.

RESURRECTION EGGS

 Time duration: 30 minutes

You will need: twelve plastic Easter eggs, the type that come apart in the centre (available from the Internet or craft shops) and a double egg box (twelve cups) in which to store the filled eggs.

To fill the eggs, you will need a toy donkey, a coin, a small cup, praying hands, a leather strip, crown of thorns, nails, a dice, a small spear (cut from card and covered with tin foil, or a toy sword from a toy soldier), a piece of gauze, a small stone.

If you prefer, complete resurrection egg kits are available on the Internet, containing eggs, artefacts and the box to keep them in.

Hand the eggs out to the children, but ask them not to open them yet. Ask the children to bring each egg to the front in turn as the story progresses. Make sure you can identify in which order the eggs need to be opened.

Ask the children what they think might be inside before each egg is opened (particularly in the case of the last egg, which is empty). Open each egg before you tell the related portion of the story. Ask the children how the object might be relevant to the story, and let them talk about it if they wish. Then read the story. After the story, offer any appropriate comments, possibly by asking a question.

1. Palm Sunday

MATTHEW 21:1–9
Your object in an egg is a toy donkey.

Here are some questions to ask with the story.

* How did Jesus enter Jerusalem?
* Has anyone heard the words 'Blessed is he who comes in the name of the Lord'? The words the crowd shouted are still said today in church.
* What is the Sunday before Easter called? We celebrate the Sunday before Easter Day as Palm Sunday, when the crowd cut palm branches from the trees to welcome Jesus.

Read the following story from the Bible, or retell it in your own words.

When Jesus and his disciples came near Jerusalem, he went to Bethphage on the Mount of Olives and sent two of them on ahead. He told them, 'Go into the next village, where you will at once find a donkey and her colt. Untie the two donkeys and bring them to me. If anyone asks why you are doing that, just say, 'The Lord needs them.' Straight away he will let you have the donkeys.' … The disciples left and did what Jesus had told them to do. They brought the donkey and its colt and laid some clothes on their backs. Then Jesus got on. Many people spread clothes in the road, while others put down branches which they had cut from trees. Some people walked ahead of Jesus and others followed behind. They were all shouting, 'Hooray for the Son of David! God bless the one who comes in the name of the Lord. Hooray for God in heaven above!'

The scribes and Pharisees did not like the welcome Jesus had received. They plotted together to arrest and kill Jesus.

2. Judas and the chief priests

MATTHEW 26:14–16
Your object in an egg is a coin.

Here are some questions to ask with the story.

★ Which disciple betrayed Jesus?
★ Why do you think he did this?

Read the following story from the Bible, or retell it in your own words.

Judas Iscariot was one of the twelve disciples. He went to the chief priests and asked, 'How much will you give me if I help you arrest

Jesus?' They paid Judas thirty silver coins, and from then on he started looking for a good chance to betray Jesus.

3. Jesus eats the Passover meal with his disciples

MATTHEW 26:17–19 AND 26–28
Your object in an egg is a cup.

Here are some questions to ask with the story.

☆ I wonder why there is a cup in this part of the story?
☆ I wonder what the name of the festival was that the Jews were celebrating at that time?
☆ In what way do we still remember Jesus' last meal with his friends in church today?

Read the following story from the Bible, or retell it in your own words.

On the first day of the Festival of Thin Bread, Jesus' disciples came to him and asked, 'Where do you want us to prepare the Passover meal?' Jesus told them to go to a certain man in the city and tell him, 'Our teacher says, "My time has come! I want to eat the Passover meal with my disciples in your home."' They did as Jesus told them and prepared the meal… During the meal Jesus took some bread in his hands. He blessed the bread and broke it. Then he gave it to his disciples and said, 'Take this and eat it. This is my body.' Jesus picked up a cup of wine and gave thanks to God. He then gave it to his disciples and said, 'Take this and drink it. This is my blood, and with it God makes his agreement with you. It will be poured out, so that many people will have their sins forgiven.'

4. Jesus prays

MARK 14:32–42
Your object in an egg is praying hands.

Here are some questions to ask with the story.

* ☆ I wonder why there are hands in this egg? What are they doing?
* ☆ I wonder if the disciples must have been tired? They couldn't stay awake even when Jesus asked them to.
* ☆ I wonder why Jesus was praying? He knew he was going to be crucified—but he was prepared to let it happen because it was what God wanted.

Read the following story from the Bible, or retell it in your own words.

Jesus went with his disciples to a place called Gethsemane, and he told them, 'Sit here while I pray.' Jesus took along Peter, James, and John. He was sad and troubled and told them, 'I am so sad that I feel as if I am dying. Stay here and keep awake with me.' Jesus walked on a little way. Then he knelt down on the ground and prayed, 'Father, if it is possible, don't let this happen to me! Father, you can do anything. Don't make me suffer by having me drink from this cup. But do what you want, and not what I want.' When Jesus came back and found the disciples sleeping, he said to Simon Peter, 'Are you asleep? Can't you stay awake for just one hour? Stay awake and pray that you won't be tested. You want to do what is right, but you are weak.' Jesus went back and prayed the same prayer. But when he returned to the disciples, he found them sleeping again. They simply could not keep their eyes open, and they did not know what to say. When Jesus returned to the disciples the third time, he said, 'Are you still sleeping and resting? Enough of that! The time has come for the Son of Man to be handed over to sinners. Get up! Let's go. The one who will betray me is already here.'

As Jesus spoke, soldiers arrived to arrest him. Judas had told them where Jesus was. Jesus was handed over to Pontius Pilate, who questioned him but could not find that he had done anything wrong. However, the people had been influenced by the chief priests and did not want Jesus to be freed.

5. Jesus is beaten with a whip

JOHN 19:1
Your object in an egg is a leather strip.

Here are some questions to ask with the story.

✫ I wonder what this leather strip reminds us of?

Read the following story from the Bible, or retell it in your own words.

Pilate gave orders for Jesus to be beaten with a whip.

6. Jesus is sentenced to death

JOHN 19:2–16A
Your object in an egg is a crown of thorns.

Here are some questions to ask with the story.

✫ I wonder what this might be?
✫ Why do you think people were laughing at Jesus? They made him suffer even more by making fun of him.
✫ Who knows what 'crucify him' means? Crucifixion is very cruel.

Read the following story from the Bible, or retell it in your own words.

The soldiers made a crown out of thorn branches and put it on Jesus. Then they put a purple robe on him. They came up to him and said, 'Hey, you king of the Jews!' They also hit him with their fists. Once again Pilate went out. This time he said, 'I will have Jesus brought out to you again. Then you can see for yourselves that I have not found him guilty.' Jesus came out, wearing the crown of thorns and the purple robe... When the chief priests and the temple police saw him, they yelled, 'Nail him to a cross! Nail him to a cross!' Pilate told them, 'You take him and nail him to a cross! I don't find him guilty of anything.' The crowd replied, 'He claimed to be the Son of God! Our Jewish Law says that he must be put to death.' When Pilate heard this, he was terrified... It was about midday on the day before Passover, and Pilate said to the crowd, 'Look at your king!' 'Kill him! Kill him!' they yelled. 'Nail him to a cross!' 'So you want me to nail your king to a cross?' Pilate asked. The chief priests replied, 'The Emperor is our king!' Then Pilate handed Jesus over to be nailed to a cross.

7. Jesus is nailed to a cross

JOHN 19:16B–22
Your objects in an egg are nails.

Here are some questions to ask with the story.

★ I wonder what these nails could be for?
★ The cross is a very important symbol. I wonder if we can see any in our church? (The crosses in your church may be covered on Good Friday.)

Read the following story from the Bible, or retell it in your own words.

Jesus was taken away, and he carried his cross to a place known as 'The Skull'. In Aramaic this place is called 'Golgotha'. There Jesus was nailed to the cross, and on each side of him a man was also nailed to a cross. Pilate ordered the charge against Jesus to be written on a board and put above the cross. It read, 'Jesus of Nazareth, King of the Jews.' The words were written in Hebrew, Latin, and Greek. The place where Jesus was taken wasn't far from the city, and many of the Jewish people read the charge against him. So the chief priests went to Pilate and said, 'Why did you write that he is King of the Jews? You should have written, "He claimed to be King of the Jews."' But Pilate told them, 'What is written will not be changed!'

8. The soldiers gamble for Jesus' robe, and Jesus dies

JOHN 19:23–25 AND MATTHEW 27:45–51
Your object in an egg is a dice.

Here are some questions to ask with the story.

☆ What do we do with dice?
☆ Why do you think the soldiers were playing a game while Jesus was dying?

Read the following story from the Bible, or retell it in your own words.

After the soldiers had nailed Jesus to the cross, they divided up his clothes into four parts, one for each of them. But his outer garment was made from a single piece of cloth, and it did not have any seams. The soldiers said to each other, 'Let's not rip it apart. We will gamble to see who gets it.' … The soldiers then did what they had decided. Jesus' mother stood beside his cross with her sister and Mary the wife of Clopas. Mary Magdalene was standing there too.

At midday the sky turned dark and stayed that way until three o'clock. Then about that time Jesus shouted, 'Eli, Eli, lema sabachthani?' which means, 'My God, my God, why have you deserted me?' Some of the people standing there heard Jesus and said, He's calling for Elijah.' … Once again Jesus shouted, and then he died. At once the curtain in the temple was torn in two from top to bottom. The earth shook, and rocks split apart.

Pause

9. The soldiers make sure Jesus is really dead

> JOHN 19:32–34
> Your object in an egg is a small spear.

Here are some questions to ask with the story.

★ What did the soldiers do with the spear?
★ Why couldn't bodies be left on the crosses on the Sabbath?

Read the following story from the Bible, or retell it in your own words.

The soldiers first broke the legs of the other two men who were nailed there. But when they came to Jesus, they saw that he was already dead, and they did not break his legs. One of the soldiers stuck his spear into Jesus' side, and blood and water came out.

10. Jesus is buried

> MATTHEW 27:57–61
> Your object in an egg is a piece of gauze.

Here are some questions to ask with the story:

★ What might this material be for?
★ I wonder why Joseph of Arimathea offered his tomb?

Read the following story from the Bible, or retell it in your own words.

That evening a rich disciple named Joseph from the town of Arimathea went and asked for Jesus' body. Pilate gave orders for it to be given to Joseph, who took the body and wrapped it in a clean linen cloth. Then Joseph put the body in his own tomb that had been cut into solid rock and had never been used. He rolled a big stone against the entrance to the tomb and went away. All this time Mary Magdalene and the other Mary were sitting across from the tomb.

11. On Sunday morning

MATTHEW 28:1–2
Your object in an egg is a stone.

Here is a question to ask with the story.

★ What was the stone used for?

Read the following story from the Bible, or retell it in your own words.

The Sabbath was over, and it was almost daybreak on Sunday when Mary Magdalene and the other Mary went to see the tomb. Suddenly a strong earthquake struck, and the Lord's angel came down from heaven. He rolled away the stone and sat on it.

12. Jesus is alive

MATTHEW 28:5–10
Your egg is empty.

Here are some questions to ask with the story.

★ What do you think will be in this egg? (before opening)
★ Why is it empty?

Read the following story from the Bible, or retell it in your won words.

The angel said to the women, 'Don't be afraid! I know you are looking for Jesus, who was nailed to a cross. He isn't here! God has raised him to life, just as Jesus said he would. Come, see the place where his body was lying. Now hurry! Tell his disciples that he has been raised to life and is on his way to Galilee. Go there, and you will see him. That is what I came to tell you.' The women were frightened and yet very happy, as they hurried from the tomb and ran to tell his disciples. Suddenly Jesus met them and greeted them. They went near him, held on to his feet, and worshipped him. Then Jesus said, 'Don't be afraid! Tell my followers to go to Galilee. They will see me there.'

THE DREAM OF THE ROOD

Another way to tell the story is by using the poem 'The Dream of the Rood'. It contains a very powerful image of the cross, first running with blood and gore and then being miraculously transformed into a glittering image studded with precious stones. The version used here has been adapted from the original Old English poem carved on the Ruthwell Cross and has been abridged to make it more accessible for children. The poem lends itself to an instrumental accompaniment. The children could make their own instruments, or instruments could be provided for them to play.

First of all, read the poem to the children and talk about it. Get the children to decide which instruments give the right sound at the right place in the poem. Practise the poem a few times with the instruments being played at the appropriate places. Younger children will need quite a lot of help with this, but the end result is very worthwhile. The piece can be performed to the parents at the end of the session or perhaps to the wider congregation during an Easter service in church.

Part One

Use bells, tinkling instruments, elastic band zithers, milk bottles and so on.

Listen, and I'll tell you about the most wonderful dream
Which came to me in the middle of the night.
It was as though I saw the most amazing tree
Touching the sky with light shining from it,
The tree was covered with gold and studded with precious stones.
It was no cross for criminals, but angels, people and
All kinds of animals, birds and other creatures
Gazed at the glorious tree.

Part Two

Use elastic double bass, twanging instruments, scraping sounds. (When the line 'Speckled with blood/bedecked with treasure' is read, all the instruments are played in an alternating pattern.)

Then I began to see behind that gold
The quarrels long ago of wretched people, as
On its right side the cross began to bleed.
I was full of sorrow, and very much afraid.
I saw the tree changing its appearance;
Sometimes it was speckled with blood and drenched with flowing gore,
At other times it was bedecked with treasure.
So I lay there watching the Saviour's tree, for a long, long time.

Then it spoke these words to me:

Part Three

On the words 'cut down', use woodblocks. On the word 'hurrying', use shakers. On the word 'trembled', use cardboard sheets rumbling. On the word 'pierced', use woodblocks.

A long time ago I was cut down at the edge of the wood.
Wicked people took me.
They made me a spectacle to punish their criminals.
They carried me to a hill, and fastened me there.
And then I saw Jesus, the Lord of all humankind
Hurrying, eager to climb up upon me.
I did not dare bend down or break against God's word.
I saw all the surface of the earth tremble and shake.
Although I could have struck down all his enemies,
Instead I stood I firm while Jesus, determined and strong in heart,
Climbed on to the cross which was me, to redeem humankind.
He embraced me and I trembled but still did not dare to bend.
I held high the Lord of heaven and dared not stoop.
They pierced me with dark nails; but still I might
Not harm them. I was soaked with the blood
Which poured out from his side.

Part Four

Use sad-sounding instruments: elastic double bass, scraping instruments, hollow sounds, cardboard rumble sound. On the words 'They took up Jesus and lifted him from his heavy torture', keep silence. On the words 'They carved it of bright stone' and 'But I remained there weeping', use woodblocks.

Darkness covered the Lord's corpse,
Shadows passed across his shining beauty
All creation wept;
Christ was on the cross.
Then I saw people hurrying to us from afar.
They took up Jesus and lifted him from his heavy torture.
He rested there a while. The people then made a tomb for him.
They carved it of bright stone and put the Lord of victories inside
And then they went away.
But I remained there weeping while the Lord's body grew cold.

Part Five

No instruments are needed. Silence is maintained while Part Five is read.

> *I have suffered at the hands of wicked people*
> *And yet now over all the earth I am honoured.*
> *Once I was the cruellest of tortures,*
> *Most hateful to everyone until on me the Lord*
> *Opened the right way of life for everyone.*
> *And now you must share this vision with humankind.*

TELLING THE STORY USING GODLY PLAY

If you wish, you could tell the Easter story using *Godly Play* (see page 189 for details of resources).

DISPLAYS FOR THE CHURCH

EASTER TABLEAUX

Developing and practising a series of tableaux for performance on Easter Day, or even when the parents collect the children, can be an excellent way of getting the older children to engage with the Easter story. You will need to rehearse how each scene will look and how the children will move from one scene to the next. Keep costumes and props as simple as possible.

EASTER GARDENS

Obtain a sizeable wooden board and use papier mâché and paint to provide the bare bones of an Easter garden (a tomb, the crosses and so on). Ask the children to complete the garden. They might find moss, grass and wild flowers in the churchyard. Remind them not to pick all the flowers they find, and not to take any from graves. If Easter is early or flowers in your churchyard are few, you will need to use shop-bought flowers.

Once the garden has been completed for the display in the church, give each child a plastic plate and invite them to put together their own Easter garden to take home.

CARDBOARD BOX CROSS COLLAGE

 Time duration: 30 minutes

You will need: cardboard boxes (preferably all the same size: half case of wine size is ideal), strong adhesive, masking tape, newspaper, PVA glue, brown or white emulsion paint, corrugated cardboard, sheets of black paper (one per child), red poster paint, paintbrushes, gold or metallic paper, lots of bright sparkly materials, such as glitter glue, sequins, fake jewellery and so on.

This collage is very effective for displaying in church after your workshop and fits well with a 'sadness turning to joy' theme in general and the poem 'The Dream of the Rood' in particular. Although the activity does take some initial preparation, it's really worthwhile.

Re-seal the boxes by gluing them shut, then stack them together to form a cross shape and glue them using good strong glue (for example, Thixofix). You may need to wait for the vertical part to dry before adding the horizontal arms. Put masking tape over the joints to smooth them out.

Next, paste newspaper over the cross for both strength and smoothness. You could also paint it with emulsion if you wanted to be sure of covering up the newsprint.

You will probably need to glue the cross on to a platform of thick corrugated card or a larger box at the base to give it some stability.

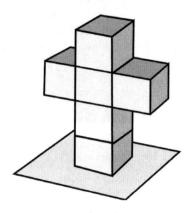

During the workshop, talk about how Jesus died and give each child some black paper. Lay out red paint and brushes. Ask them to make a picture about the crucifixion. When these are dry, they can be stuck on to one side of the cross.

Also ask the children to make a picture showing the joy of the resurrection. Give them gold or metallic paper and lots of bright sparkly materials to make their picture, such as glitter glue, sequins, fake jewellery and so on. Stick these pictures on to the other side of the cross.

The children could then do pictures showing a Station or Stations of the Cross (bring some examples to show them). These can be stuck round the edges of the cardboard box cross.

Display the cross with the red and gory side facing the congregation on Good Friday. It can then be turned round so that everyone can see the glittery side on Easter Day.

GIANT CROSS MOSAIC

 Time duration: 15 minutes

You will need: heavyweight black A2 card (to use as a collage board) *or* collage board covered with black sugar paper or thin card, drawing materials, colour pictures from magazines, coloured paper, sandpaper in different grades, containers to hold the mosaic paper, glue and glue spreaders.

This makes a fantastic collage picture, which can be displayed in church. Before the session, cover a collage board with black sugar paper or thin card. Next, draw an outline of your design on to it (for example, a large cross in the foreground, on a green hill, with desert and sky in the background).

You will then need to make the mosaic pieces by cutting colour pictures from magazines. Decide roughly how big the mosaic pieces will be (depending on the size of your completed picture) and cut the magazine pictures into coloured squares. There is no need for the squares to be accurately sized. Squares of different-grade sandpaper are very effective for the cross itself. Sort the different colours together in containers so that they are easy to find and use.

Provide the children with glue and spreaders, tell them how they need to put the picture together and let them get on with it.

This is a useful activity for Good Friday, but it can be extended to the Easter Day service too. When you are cutting squares for the mosaic, look for pictures of flowers and cut some of these out. On Easter Day, perhaps as part of the intercessions or during a hymn, adult (and child) members of the congregation can come up and stick flowers over the cross.

CARDBOARD TUBE SHEEP

 Time duration: 10 minutes

You will need: one cardboard tube for each sheep to be made, scissors, PVA glue, cotton wool, black felt cut to shape for sheep faces and feet, googly eyes (optional).

Cut through the tube lengthways and then cut a semicircle out from each side of the cut edge. This will leave you with a rounded back of an animal and four legs. Ease out the 'legs' so that the sheep can stand up. Set out glue and cotton wool and get each child to cover their sheep with cotton wool. Have some pre-cut small felt squares for the feet and a face and ears shape. Googly eyes could be applied to the face for even better effect.

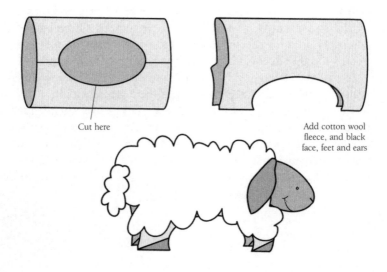

Cut here

Add cotton wool
fleece, and black
face, feet and ears

EASTER BASKETS

 Time duration: 10 minutes

You will need: lightweight card, paper doilies, scissors, glue.

Cut out two circles of card for each basket to be made. Fold each one in half and fit them together to form a basket. Line each basket with paper doily and add a handle cut from a strip of matching paper.

THIS ACTIVITY IS ADAPTED FROM ONE IN *HERE'S ONE I MADE EARLIER* BY KATHRYN COPSEY (SCRIPTURE UNION).

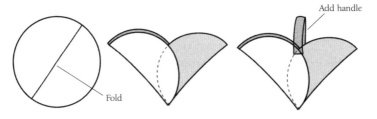

Add handle

Fold

SPRINGY SHEEP CARDS

 Time duration: 15 minutes

You will need: lightweight white card, lightweight black card, coloured card to form the main body of the card, scissors, glue, googly eyes, pencils.

You will need to pre-cut sheep body shapes from white card (see template on page 187). Colour the head, ears and legs black. Assemble the sheep, adding googly eyes if you have any. Then concertina-fold a strip of card and glue it to the back of the sheep. Glue the other end of the concertina to a folded piece of coloured card, either on the front or inside. Write an Easter message.

SAD-TO-HAPPY DOLLS

 Time duration: 10 minutes

You will need: a wooden spoon for each child, gel marker pens, scraps of wool, scraps of fabric, scissors, glue.

Give each child a wooden spoon and ask them to draw a happy face on the back and a sad face on the bowl of the spoon. They can stick on lengths of wool for hair and attach the 'clothing', using dabs of glue to fix everything in place.

SAD-TO-HAPPY MEDALS

 Time duration: 10 minutes

You will need: mediumweight card, tin foil, blunt pencils or ballpoint pens, scraps of ribbon, large safety pins, glue.

You will need to cut some card circles to make the medals (each medal will need two circles). Also have some foil cut so that it is larger than the circles and can be wrapped round them. Have some ribbons already made up to look like medal ribbons and safety pins large enough to fit round the ribbon.

The children will need to smooth the square of foil round a card circle. Do this twice so each child has two foil-covered disks. Give them blunt pencils or ballpoint pens and ask them to draw a happy face on the foil-covered side of one disk, and a sad face on the other.

The disks can be glued together with the ribbon in between the two disks and the safety pin inside the ribbon so that the medal can be pinned to the child's clothing. The children can wear the medals with the sad side facing out on Good Friday and the happy face showing on Easter Sunday.

EASTER BONNETS

 Time duration: 10 minutes

You will need: strips of thin card large enough to fit round each child's head *and/or* dinner plate-sized circles of thin card with a slit cut from the outside to the centre so that you can form a cone shape to make a hat, glue, items for decoration, such as painted pasta, fake jewels, holographic paper shapes, tissue paper, tin foil and so on.

Give the children plenty of glue and items for decoration, and let them create their Easter bonnets.

PAINTED STONES

 Time duration: 10 minutes

You will need: cobble stones (one per child), poster paints, brushes.

You can use this activity to talk about how Jesus' body was buried in the tomb with the stone sealing the entrance. Give the children a dry, dust-free cobble stone each (you can buy them in garden centres) and set out paint and brushes. Suggest that they paint their stone to look like an animal. They will be making the stones look alive, but Jesus really did come alive and gave life to us too when he rose from the dead.

Time duration: 10 minutes

You will need: plastic containers (one per child), medium-weight card, scissors, plastic vegetable trays or plastic plates, kitchen paper, packets of cress seeds, water.

Decide how big the containers will be into which the children will sow their cress. Then cut out a few cross-shaped stencils from thick card.

Give each child a shallow tray or plastic plate and some kitchen paper. Dampen the kitchen paper. Then let them sow their cress seeds through the cross-shaped stencil.

Children may need help so as not to sow the seeds too thickly and, when taking the stencil away, so as not to drop seeds outside the cross shape. When the cress grows, it should make a green cross cross.

COOKING FOR EASTER

MAKING BREAD

Children always enjoy making bread. You can either make it from scratch or have some ready-made bread dough for the children to shape into rolls. (You will find a recipe on page 177.) It's a nice idea to use one of their rolls for the next service of holy communion in church.

If you have a bread machine, you could either plug it in at church or use it to make dough in advance, ready for shaping later by the children. Dough will keep in plastic bags in the fridge overnight, though the bread may take longer to prove once it is shaped and before baking.

EASTER BISCUITS

You will find the recipe for the biscuit mix on page 176. Divide the dough into enough pieces for each child. Have a surface ready for rolling: pieces of well-floured baking parchment or greaseproof paper on your normal table covering work well and are disposable later. The dough should be rolled out to about 5mm thickness and then the biscuits can be cut out.

Get each child to place their biscuits on a named piece of baking parchment. Bake in an oven pre-heated to Gas Mark 3 or 160°C for about 18 minutes.

Try to find cutters that match your theme, such as sheep-shaped cutters for the good shepherd theme, or crosses.

As with any food activity, check whether any of the children have allergies. As this biscuit recipe contains egg, make sure they don't eat the raw dough. You will need hand-washing facilities for before and after this activity; if you have no water connection, a plastic washing-up bowl, water warmed in a kettle, some soap and towels will do just as well.

The biscuits could be taken home in Easter baskets (see p. 91).

GAMES FOR EASTER

KIM'S GAME

 Time duration: 15 minutes

You will need: a tray and a cloth to cover it, items associated with the Easter story such as coins, vinegar, small sword (perhaps from a toy soldier), dice, bread, wine, palm leaf, nails, stone, thorny twigs, linen and so on, A4 paper (one sheet per child), pencils.

Talk with the children about each item and where it fits into the Easter story, then cover the tray and see how many the children can remember within a time limit of, say, one minute. If the children are too young to write the items down, just ask them to tell you what they remember.

PRAYERS FOR EASTER

PRAYER STONES

On Good Friday, give a stone to each child and ask them to pray while holding the stone and thinking of Jesus' death and resurrection. (You might need to talk to them about what not to do with stones before you hand them out.)

EASTER PRAYERS

Sit the children in a circle, then pass around objects from the Kim's game activity so that the children can pray over each one before passing it on.

Theme 7

AFTER EASTER

It is easy to see Easter Day as the conclusion of the Easter story and forget to look beyond to the resurrection accounts of the risen Jesus. These stories can yield some rewarding activities for a workshop and it's good for the children to realize that there is a period of time celebrated by the church during the 50 days between Easter and Pentecost.

STORIES FOR AFTER EASTER

Stories that work well for children include 'On the road to Emmaus', 'Jesus and Thomas' and 'The barbecue on the beach'. It is good when telling more than one story in a workshop to vary the storytelling technique. The following programme tells the Emmaus road story while taking the children on a short walk, uses feely boxes for the story of Jesus and Thomas, and audience participation for the story of the barbeque on the beach.

ON THE ROAD TO EMMAUS

LUKE 24:13–35

Take the children for a walk, but, before the session, prepare by placing some chairs and a table, laid with a cloth and some bread, halfway round the route. The walk could be round the churchyard if the weather is fine or inside the church if it's raining.

First stop (the church porch): On the first Easter day, two of Jesus' friends were going to a town named Emmaus. As they were walking along, they were talking about everything that had happened to Jesus…

Second stop (the west door): While they were walking, Jesus came near and began walking with them. But they did not recognize him. He said, 'What are you talking about?' They stopped. They were very sad and said, 'You must be the only person in Jerusalem who doesn't know what has happened there.' Jesus said, 'What do you mean?'

Third stop (a landmark along the route): The two friends told their companion about Jesus of Nazareth: how he was a prophet, how he had said and done so many wonderful things and how he had been betrayed and killed by being nailed to a cross. They told him how that very day (the first Easter Day) some of their friends had told them that Jesus' body had gone from the tomb and were saying that he was alive again.

Fourth stop (the east end of north wall): Jesus said to them, 'You should believe all that the prophets said—that the Christ must suffer before he enters his glory.' Then Jesus began to explain everything that had been written about himself in the scriptures.

Fifth stop (the east window): As they came near to Emmaus, the two friends asked Jesus to stay with them, as it was getting late. So Jesus went with them to their house.

Sixth stop (the table laid with a cloth and the bread): Jesus sat down with them, took some bread and thanked God for the food. Then he broke the bread and shared it with them. As he broke the bread, they recognized him. But when they realized who he was, he disappeared. Then they got up and ran back to Jerusalem, even though it was late, to find the disciples and other friends of Jesus to tell them that Jesus really had risen from the dead.

Seventh stop (return to the porch): Talk about why the two disciples walking to Emmaus may not have recognized Jesus. Relate the discussion to how we sometimes don't recognize friends or people we know well simply if we're not expecting to see them, or if they appear wearing different clothes or in a different car or even just in different places from where we usually see them.

JESUS AND THOMAS

JOHN 20:19–29

 Time duration: 10 minutes

You will need: four feely boxes containing the following items:
* ☆ Box One: keys (locked room)
* ☆ Box Two: nails (nail marks in Jesus' hands)
* ☆ Box Three: bread (Jesus' body)
* ☆ Box Four: empty (even if we can't see or touch Jesus, it doesn't mean he's not present)

Hand out Box One: On the evening of the first Easter day, Jesus' disciples were together. The doors were locked because they were afraid of the Jewish authorities. Suddenly, Jesus came and stood among them and said, 'Peace be with you!' Then he showed them his hands and his side. The disciples were very happy when they saw Jesus, but one of the disciples, Thomas, wasn't present when this event took place.

Hand out Box Two: When the other disciples told Thomas that they had seen Jesus, he refused to believe them. He said, 'I will not believe until I see the nail marks in his hands. I will not believe until I put my finger on the scars where the nails were and put my hand into his side.'

Hand out Box Three: A week later the disciples were together again, but this time Thomas was with them. The doors were locked, but Jesus came and stood among them. He said, 'Peace be with you.' Then he said to Thomas, 'Put your finger here. Look at my hands. Put your hand here in my side. Stop doubting and believe.'

Hand out Box Four: Thomas said to Jesus, 'You are my Lord and my God.' Then Jesus said to Thomas, 'You have faith because you have seen me. The people who have faith in me without seeing me are the ones who are really blessed!'

THE BARBECUE ON THE BEACH

JOHN 21:1–14

This story is told with actions and sound effects as follows.

* ☆ At the word 'fish', the children make fish movements with their hands.
* ☆ At the word 'net', the children make net shapes with their fingers.
* ☆ At the word 'Jesus', the children shout 'Alleluia'.
* ☆ At the word 'water', the children shout 'Splash'.

After he was risen, *Jesus* appeared to his disciples by Lake Galilee. It happened like this.

Some of the disciples were together and Peter said, 'I'm going fishing.' The other disciples said, 'We will go with you.' So they all got into the boat, pushed it out into the *water* and went fishing. But they did not catch any *fish*.

Early the next morning *Jesus* stood on the shore, but the disciples did not realize that it was him. *Jesus* called out to them, 'Friends, have you caught any *fish*?' They answered, 'No!'

Jesus said, 'Throw your *net* into the *water* on the right side of the boat and you will catch some *fish*.' They did this and they caught so many *fish* that they could not pull the *net* back into the boat.

One of the disciples said to Peter, 'It is *Jesus*!' When Peter heard this, he jumped into the *water* and swam to the shore. The others followed in the boat, dragging the *net* full of *fish*. When they got to the shore, they saw a fire of hot coals. There were *fish* on the fire and there was bread to eat.

Then *Jesus* said, 'Bring some of the *fish* that you caught.' Peter went to the boat and pulled the *net* through the *water* to the shore. It was full of big *fish*. There were 153. But even though there were so many *fish*, the *net* had not torn. *Jesus* said to them, 'Come and eat.' None of the disciples dared to ask 'Who are you?' They knew it was *Jesus*. *Jesus* came and took the bread and gave it to them. He also gave them the *fish*.

DISPLAYS FOR THE CHURCH

FOOTPRINTS PAINTING

 Time duration: 20 minutes

You will need: a long roll of ordinary, but reasonably heavy-duty lining paper, polythene sheeting, large paintbrushes, water-based paint in a selection of colours, soap, warm water and towels.

Protect the floor with polythene sheeting, unless it is dry and warm enough to do this activity outside. Have one adult helper at one end of the paper with paint and brushes, and another at the other end with foot-washing equipment.

Get the children to remove their shoes and socks. They can then have their feet painted in whichever colour they choose. Each child then walks or dances down the paper to the other end. When they've finished leaving footprints on the paper, their feet will need to be washed and dried.

This should make a long, thin picture that can be put on display or used as the background to other displays.

FISH TANK

Time duration: 20 minutes

You will need: mediumweight card, tissue paper in a variety of colours, tin foil, PVA glue and glue spreaders, a cardboard box with the top and two sides cut away and decorated to look like the sea, small garden canes, thread.

This works well with the story of the barbecue on the beach. Get the children to stick tissue paper and foil strips on to the card. When their work is dry, cut the card into fish shapes (see template on page 187). Make cuts through the fish to produce a three-dimensional effect. Lay the garden canes across the top of the fish tank and, using the thread, suspend the fish from the canes to complete the fish tank.

CRAFTS FOR AFTER EASTER

WAX CANDLE DRAWINGS

Time duration: 10 minutes

You will need: decorative paper (smooth but in good colours), household candles (softened in some warm water), ink or watery paint, brushes.

This activity is designed to go with the story of Jesus and Thomas. The children need to draw a picture by pressing hard with the candles. They will not be able to see the picture, but when they paint over it with the ink, the paper without the wax will take up the ink, revealing the wax drawing.

Explain that even though they couldn't see the picture, it was still there. Although Thomas didn't see Jesus when he first appeared, the resurrection had still taken place and he was alive again.

GAMES FOR AFTER EASTER

WHO AM I?

 Time duration: 20 minutes

You will need: small pieces of card.

For older children, a guessing game links well to the story of the road to Emmaus. Write the names of famous people or TV characters (including cartoon characters) on the pieces of card.

Put the children into pairs. Give one child in each pair a card with a name on it. The other child has to work out what that name is by asking questions to which the first child can only answer 'yes' or 'no'.

PRAYERS FOR AFTER EASTER

RECOGNIZING JESUS

Make prayers about recognizing Jesus. Perhaps the children could write a line each of a prayer about times when we might not recognize him.

Theme 8

ASCENSION, PENTECOST AND TRINITY

The theme of Pentecost has two strands. First of all, there is the story of the first Pentecost, which gives the opportunity to explore the account in the book of Acts in detail. Secondly, Pentecost is the Church's birthday, which gives the opportunity to look at what the Church is and how we all fit into it. The festival of the Ascension and the doctrine of the Trinity fit with the Pentecost story to give a complete picture, and ideally should be included in the Pentecost workshop.

STORIES FOR ASCENSION, PENTECOST AND TRINITY

Jesus returns to heaven, the coming of the Holy Spirit and the baptism of Jesus.

LUKE 24:50–53; MARK 16:19–20; ACTS 1:9–11; ACTS 2:1–42; MATTHEW 3:13–17; MARK 1:9–11; LUKE 3:21–22

ASCENSION: JESUS RETURNS TO HEAVEN

Tell the story of the Ascension using a contemporary version of the Bible or a *Godly Play* approach (see page 189 for resources). Follow this with a discussion about how the disciples watched when Jesus was taken away and how they had to let go of him, so that he could be with all of us everywhere, all the time, in the person of the Holy Spirit.

To illustrate the 'letting go' aspect of Ascension, arrange for some balloons to be filled with helium so that they will float away. Give the children a luggage label each and ask them to write a verse from the Bible story on it and then decorate it. Attach a label to each balloon, then release the balloons outside and watch them float away. (You will need to consider the age of the children here, as younger ones might be unwilling to let go of their balloons.)

PENTECOST: THE COMING OF THE HOLY SPIRIT

 Time duration: 15 minutes

You will need: red and orange crêpe paper cut into streamers, a CD of joyful music, CD player.

First, practise making a collective sound of wind by breathing out with mouths open, quietly first, then loudly. Next, explain that we are going to hear about the day when God breathed his life and power into his people. Tell the story of the Pentecost using a contemporary version of the Bible or the version below:

Ten days before our story takes place, the disciples had seen Jesus taken up into heaven and had been told to wait in Jerusalem for the coming of the Holy Spirit. They had no idea what that meant or what to expect, but Jesus had told them to wait expectantly, so that is what they did.

Ask the children to all sit waiting as the disciples did that morning; waiting for the gift of God's Holy Spirit.

Suddenly there was a sound like the wind, coming from the sky and getting closer. It was the sound of God breathing his Holy Spirit into his loyal friends.

All start quiet breathing out with mouths open.

The sound got louder and louder, until the whole house they were in seemed surrounded by the living, moving presence of almighty God.

Breathe louder.

Suddenly, it seemed that tongues of flame flickered out from the breath of God and found each person, resting on each one very gently.

Children wave streamers made from red and orange crêpe paper, finally bringing them to rest on the floor.

The disciples were all filled with God's Holy Spirit. They started praising God and shouting out their love for him. They didn't care what anyone else thought of them. All they wanted to do was to thank him and tell him how much they loved him. They lifted their hands and all started talking at once.

Play some music or get the children to sing a song with gusto, dancing and waving the streamers as they do so.

Quite a crowd had gathered outside the house, wondering what was going on so early in the morning. Still full of God's Spirit, the disciples ran out to share the good news. That's what the Church, including us, has been called to do ever since—to be filled with God's living Spirit and, in our excitement and joy, run out to share the good news with all the people we meet.

Follow the story by talking about languages. Find out how to say 'Come, Holy Spirit' in a foreign language, and get the children to make up a code for the words 'Come, Holy Spirit'. Talk about how we need the 'key' to understand a different language. For a spoken language, this would be basic grammar and vocabulary; for a code, it would be the legend. When God speaks to us, the Bible helps to provide the 'key' so that we can understand what he is saying.

THE BAPTISM OF JESUS

This story paints an excellent picture of the three persons of the Trinity coming together as Jesus is affirmed and equipped for the task ahead. Tell the story using a contemporary version of the Bible or a *Godly Play* approach (see page 189 for resources). Follow this with a discussion about the ways we can illustrate the idea of God as three in one. The three parts of an egg, the three states of water and the leaf of a shamrock are good examples to use.

DISPLAYS FOR THE CHURCH

CORONATION COLLAGE

 Time duration: 25 minutes

You will need: heavyweight card (collage board), collage materials including fake jewels, metallic and holographic paper, foil and cotton wool (to make ermine trim), colouring pens and pencils, PVA glue, scissors.

For the festival of Ascension, it would be appropriate to produce a collage showing coronation paraphernalia: a crown, orb and sceptre.

Either draw the shapes on to a prepared collage board or have some pre-cut shapes that the children can decorate individually, assembling the completed picture later. Add the caption 'Jesus reigns'.

CELEBRATION BUNTING

 Time duration: 15 minutes

You will need: brightly coloured paper, collage materials, painting materials (optional), colouring materials, PVA glue, a long ball of string, scissors.

Cut diamond shapes of brightly coloured paper, so that when they are folded over they become triangles. Get the children to decorate them to form bunting. They can each decorate as many shapes as they like. The diamonds can be decorated with crayons, collage or paint (if you have time to let it dry). Let the children's imaginations run riot!

As each diamond is completed, glue it to make a double-sided triangle round the string. When the string of flags is finished, use it to decorate the church to celebrate Ascension, Pentecost or Trinity.

TRINITY BANNER

 Time duration: 20 minutes

You will need: 1 metre of fabric or a very large sheet of card, collage materials or painting materials, PVA glue.

Lay out the fabric or card and get the children to use paints or collage to make a design showing a circle divided into three segments, one for each person of the Trinity. The words 'Holy, Holy, Holy' could be incorporated into the design.

CRAFTS FOR ASCENSION, PENTECOST AND TRINITY

SELF-SCULPTURE CANDLE HOLDERS

 Time duration: 15 minutes

You will need: air-drying clay, birthday candles (these come in various sizes and the fatter or larger ones are best), or tealight candles.

With older children, give each child a reasonably sized lump of air-drying clay and ask them to make a model of their own head and shoulders. When they've completed the model, give each child a birthday candle to put into the head they have made. They can now see their own heads with a tongue of flame resting on them.

With younger children, ask each child to model a hand (if necessary, they can do this by making a hand print into some clay). Then give them a tealight candle each and ask them to sink the candle just a little into the hand so that the clay hand can hold the flame.

PENTECOST CROWNS

 Time duration: 10 minutes

You will need: thin black card (large enough to circle the child's head to make a crown), holographic or metallic card in red, orange and gold, scissors, PVA glue.

Give each child a band of card large enough to circle his or her head to make a crown. Have ready a number of flame shapes cut from holographic or metallic card in red, orange and gold. Each child then decorates their own crown with the flame shapes so that, when they put them on, they too have flames resting on their heads.

PENTECOST WINDMILLS

 Time duration: 15 minutes

You will need: card egg boxes cut into segments (five segments for each child), red, orange and gold spray paints, lolly sticks (available from craft shops or the Internet), quick-drying wood glue, scissors, Plasticine, beads, dressmaking pins.

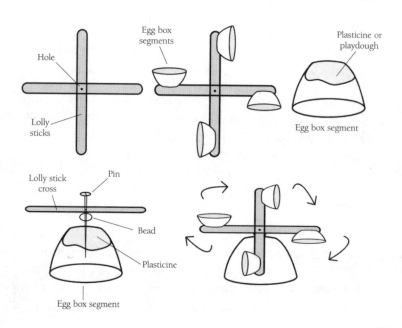

Some pre-preparation is necessary for this activity, but the result is very satisfying. Spray-paint the egg box segments in red, orange and gold colours. Paint the lolly sticks and glue them together in pairs, so that each pair forms a cross. Make a hole through the middle of the cross using a small awl.

Give each child a lolly stick cross and get them to stick an egg box segment on each arm of the cross, so that the cup parts are facing in the same direction (either clockwise or anticlockwise). Then give each child another egg box segment, cut slightly higher than the other four, and a small lump of Plasticine. Push the Plasticine into the inside of the egg box segment.

Assemble the windmill by passing a pin through the lolly stick cross, then threading a bead on to the pin and pushing the pin through the base egg box segment and Plasticine.

When the 'sails' are blown, the windmill should circulate at quite a rate.

FROM AN IDEA FROM *FUN TO MAKE* BY GILLIAN SOUTER (OFF THE SHELF PUBLISHING)

FISH WHIRLIGIG

 Time duration: 15 minutes

You will need: clean four- or six-pint plastic milk cartons, modelling knife, acrylic paints in red, orange and yellow or gold, plastic drinking straws, red insulation tape, thin garden canes, beads, Plasticine.

Cut fish shapes out of plastic milk bottle cartons, enough for each child to have three (see template on page 187). Make four triangular cuts along the body of each fish and open them out slightly. Paint one side of each fish in Pentecostal colours using acrylic paint (they will probably need two coats).

To assemble the whirligigs, give each child three fish shapes and a piece of plastic drinking straw. Tape the straw to the unpainted side of each fish with insulation tape. Thread the fish on to a garden cane, using beads and blobs of Plasticine to act as spacers between each fish so that the fish are free to spin. You may need to experiment in advance of your session to get the right diameter of bead. Alternatively, cut 'washers' from the leftover milk bottle plastic to use as spacers instead of beads. Put a lump of Plasticine over the tip of the cane to protect eyes.

When the wind (or child) blows, the fish should swing round.

PICTURING THE HOLY SPIRIT

 Time duration: 15 minutes

You will need: sheets of plain paper, drawing and colouring materials.

As well as Pentecost and the story of Jesus' baptism, tell the children other stories about how the Spirit of God is manifested in the Bible (such as the story of Moses and the burning bush in Exodus 3:1–5, or the story of Elijah on Mount Horeb in 1 Kings 19:9–13). Ask children to paint pictures of what they think the Holy Spirit might look like. You will probably be surprised at what they come up with.

HOLY SPIRIT SPINNERS

 Time duration: 10 minutes

You will need: mediumweight white card, cocktail sticks, a pair of compasses, colouring materials, Plasticine.

Cut a circle of card and make a small hole in the exact centre (if you've drawn the circle using compasses, this will be easy to find). Mark the circle into three roughly equal segments.

Give the children a circle each and get them to colour each of the three segments a different colour. Push a cocktail stick through the hole in the centre and use a small blob of Plasticine both to keep the stick in the right place and to give a bit of weight to the top to balance it. Spin the top and watch what happens to the colours: three become one.

FISH BADGES

 Time duration: 15 minutes

You will need: clean four- or six-pint plastic milk cartons, modelling knife, acrylic paints in red, orange and yellow or gold, indelible pens, safety pins, insulation tape.

Cut out the fish as instructed in the fish whirligig activity on page 111, but make only one fish per child and omit the cuts along the fish's body. Each child can then write his or her name on the fish and decorate it, if they wish, with a scale pattern, eye and gills. Turn it into a badge by sticking a safety pin on the back with some insulation tape. You could use these badges as name badges for your future sessions, too.

FISH SIGNS

 Time duration: 15 minutes

You will need: lightweight card, writing materials, scissors.

Cut out five pieces of equal-sized card. Write the Greek words below on the cards, one word on each. Write the translation on the back of its corresponding card.

Iesus / Christos / Theou / Uios / Soter
Jesus / Christ / of God / Son / Saviour

Slide the cards one over the other to make the Greek word 'Ichthus'. There may be a child in your group who is a dinosaur fan and knows about ichthyosaurs. Explain that the fish was a secret sign for the early Christians, when it was often dangerous to confess to Christian faith.

ASCENSION CANDLES

Buy sheets of beeswax in white or light colours, and lengths of candle wick. Make plain cylindrical single-colour candles using rectangular sheets of beeswax. Lay the wick along the wide edge of the beeswax sheet and roll it up with the wick inside. Cut the sheets into different shapes for different effects and use more than one colour if you wish. This activity works well with the *Godly Play* Ascension story (see page 189 for resources).

TRINITY TRIPTYCHS

 Time duration: 20 minutes

You will need: lightweight A4 card, drawing and colouring materials.

This activity is ideal for older children. Give each child a sheet of A4 card, folded widthways into three equal sections. With the paper folded, get the children to decorate the front cover and put their names on it. Then ask them to think about themselves and, inside the triptych on the left-hand section, to write some sentences about the sort of person they think they are. On the middle section, ask them to think of a member of their family (for example, a parent or sibling) and write down what they think that family member thinks about them. On the third page, they should think of a friend or someone they know and, as before, write a description of themselves from the friend's point of view.

Finish the activity by decorating the pages around the words.

CHURCH GUIDES

If you are considering producing a children's version of a church guide (see the website), Pentecost is a good time to start the project. Begin by getting the children to produce drawings of what happens in church at Pentecost. This is also a good opportunity to talk about the church as the body of Christ: we all have different gifts and a different role, but we are all necessary for the body to work properly.

COOKING FOR ASCENSION, PENTECOST AND TRINITY

CAKE DECORATING

 Time duration: 15 minutes

You will need: a large Victoria sponge cake, sandwiched with jam and covered with butter cream icing, pre-cut circles of rice paper, assorted small tubes of 'writing icing', birthday candles.

Explain that Pentecost is the Church's birthday. Have ready a huge birthday cake to cut up and share with the children and their parents and carers at the end of the session. Talk to the children about why Pentecost is the Church's birthday and explain that they are going to celebrate it.

Give each child a circle of rice paper and assorted small tubes of 'writing icing'. Ask them to decorate the circles of rice paper with faces—their own and friends' or family members' if you have enough time and a large enough cake. Stick these circles on to the cake. Add candles if there is room.

Before the cake is cut, you could sing 'Happy birthday' to 'our church'.

GAMES FOR ASCENSION, PENTECOST AND TRINITY

TRINITY TRIATHLON

 Time duration: 20 minutes

You will need: old scarves or large handkerchiefs for the three-legged race, small prizes for the winners, biscuits or sweets for the runners-up.

Divide the children into three groups. Each group has to complete each of three races: a three-legged race, a three-limb race and a three-person race. The team to complete all three races first wins a small prize. You will need biscuits or sweets as taking-part awards for everyone else! The game can be played in a hall or out of doors if the weather is fine. Designate one area as the starting point and one area as the far point of the course. The races are run between these two points.

For the three-legged race, each team gets into pairs. The first pair is tied together using a scarf or handkerchief. When they have completed their run, they untie the scarf and hand it to the second pair for their legs to be tied, and so on.

When all the team members have completed the three-legged race, each person then has to run a three-limb race in turn, completing the course using two hands and one leg to travel along.

When the team has completed the three-limb race, they then have to get into a line. The first person runs down the course and back and collects the second person. Holding hands, they both run down the hall and back and collect the third person. When these three arrive back, the next person in line becomes the first person and so on until all the team members have been collected (in groups of three) and completed the course.

PRAYERS FOR ASCENSION, PENTECOST AND TRINITY

THREE-PRONGED PRAYERS

Put three-pronged prayers together with the children. The first section might say 'Thank you, God', the next 'Thank you, Jesus' and the final one 'Thank you, Holy Spirit'.

If you are using the balloons activity (see page 105), the releasing of balloons could also be used for prayer.

Theme Nine

HARVEST

Harvest is a popular celebration and provides opportunity for lots of craft activities to help children express their thanks to God for everything they have. If you are considering fundraising for a Third World charity, this might be a good time to begin, as harvest gives us an opportunity not only to give thanks for what we have, but also to think about people who are not so fortunate.

STORIES FOR HARVEST

The story of creation, which can be found in Genesis 1:1—2:4, is an ideal story to use for harvest. There are a number of ways to tell it. The *Godly Play* approach works well, but you could also tell it using props to be distributed among the children. Make sure you have plenty of items so that everyone gets to hold at least one thing. This will also give substance to the idea of the generosity of creation.

THE STORY OF CREATION USING PROPS

 Time duration: 10 minutes

You will need: one large smiley face on a big circle of card, candle and matches, large piece of floaty blue fabric, stones and growing things such as flowers, sprigs of greenery and so on, large sun cut from gold card, large silver moon, star shapes, soft toys representing ocean creatures, birds and insects, soft toys representing land animals, large mirror.

In the beginning there was nothing… except God and perhaps an enormous smile *(hold up smiley face)*. The next time I hold up this smiley face, I need you to say 'It is good' or 'They are good'. Let's try that now… *(hold up smiley face)* 'It is good'. On with the story…

God said, 'Let there be light' *(light candle)* and there was light. God saw the light and said *(hold up smiley face)* 'It is good'. And that was the morning and the evening on the first day.

On the second day, God divided the waters above from the waters beneath and put the sky above the water *(bring out blue fabric)*. God saw the waters and the sky and said *(hold up smiley face)* 'It is good'. And that was the morning and the evening on the second day.

On the third day, God gave us the dry land *(hand out stone)*, and from the dry land he made all kinds of plants *(hand out growing things)* begin to grow: trees, bushes, herbs, flowers, weeds and crops. God saw the dry land and the growing things and said *(hold up smiley face)* 'They are good'. And that was the morning and the evening on the third day.

On the fourth day, God made the great lights in the sky: the sun which rules the day *(hand out sun)* and the moon which rules the night *(hand out moon)*, and he fixed the stars in the sky *(hand out stars)*. God saw the sun, moon and the stars and said *(hold up smiley face)* 'They are good'. And that was the morning and the evening on the fourth day.

On the fifth day, God gave us the creatures that swim in the sea—fish, whales, lobsters, jellyfish *(hand out toy lobster or whatever you have)*—and the birds that fly in the air—swallows, blackbirds, vultures, nightingales, parrots (*hand out toy parrot and so on*). God saw the creatures of the sea and the creatures of the air and said (*hold up smiley face*) 'They are good'. And that was the morning and the evening on the fifth day.

On the sixth day, God made the creatures that walk on the land, all the animals—lions, cats, dogs, mice, bears, duck-billed platypuses (*hand out lion and so on*)—and then God made people, who looked like he did (*hold up mirror*). God saw all the animals and the people and said (*hold up smiley face*) 'They are good'. God looked at all that he had made and said (*hold up smiley face*) 'They are good'. They are all very good. And that was the morning and the evening on the sixth day.

On the seventh day, God rested and said that we should have a day to rest, too, so that we can remember the glory of all God's work on the other six days.

DISPLAYS FOR THE CHURCH

HARVEST COLLAGE

 Time duration: 15 minutes

You will need: prepared collage board, collage materials including coloured paper, tissue paper, magazine pictures and so on, PVA glue.

This activity can be arranged so that the children make their collage directly on to the finished board. Alternatively, if you have a larger group of children, give them items to form the finished picture, so that each child can collage one item to be fixed on to the final picture. For example, you could cut out a series of fruit or vegetable shapes and ask each child to make a collage of one of them.

FABRIC PRINTING BANNER

 Time duration: 15 minutes

You will need: prepared fabric banner, fabric paint, brushes, variety of fruits and vegetables cut in half.

Have prepared a large piece of fabric to be used as a banner (see page 180). You will need to think about how it will be hung or displayed, so in addition to hemming the rough edges, you may need to make a casing to take a pole from which it can be hung.

Provide a number of different fruits and vegetables all cut in half (cut some lengthways as well as crossways). Invite the children to apply fabric paint to the halves of fruit and vegetables, and use them to make as many prints on the banner as they like. Older children might wish to use the prints to form a message such as 'Thank you'.

COLLAGE LETTERS BANNER

 Time duration: 30 minutes

You will need: prepared fabric banner, A5 coloured card (one for each letter of the message), PVA glue and spreaders, string, dried foods such as rice, lentils, split peas, pasta shapes or seeds, containers for dried foods.

Prepare a basic fabric banner as for the previous activity, then decide what message you'd like (for example, 'Thank you, God'). Make the phrase long enough for each child to be able to make at least one letter.

Invite the children to make a collage letter on sheets of different coloured A5 card by gluing on string to outline the letter, and dried foods to make patterns to fill in the letters. Apply the dried foods in the same way as you would glitter, shaking any loose stuff on to some paper, from where it can be tipped back into the pot or saucer).

CRAFTS FOR HARVEST

FRUIT AND VEGETABLE PEOPLE

 Time duration: 15 minutes

You will need: a variety of firm vegetables or fruit, such as potatoes, carrots, parsnips, apples and so on, pipe cleaners, Plasticine or play dough (check that it will stick to the produce).

Ask each child to choose a fruit or vegetable and turn it into a character using the pipe cleaners and modelling materials. Pipe cleaners can be pushed into the vegetable or fruit to make legs. Eyes, ears, mouth, hair, and other features can be modelled from the play dough or Plasticine and stuck to the produce.

FLOWER ARRANGING

 Time duration: 15 minutes

You will need: small plastic pots such as disposable dessert bowls (one per child), flowers (from the garden, a market stall or supermarket), oasis chopped into small blocks to fit the plastic pots, water, scissors to trim stalks.

On the whole, even boys enjoy flower arranging. Invite the children to make small flower arrangements. You will need to ensure that everyone gets a fair share of the choicest flowers.

If you are planning to get the wider community involved in your sessions, or even just the wider church community, this would be a good opportunity to invite either a regular church flower arranger or someone from your local horticultural society, women's institute or flower arranging guild to talk to the children and help them with this activity.

MODELLING HARVEST PRODUCE

 Time duration: 10 minutes

You will need: play dough or modelling clay, modelling tools (optional).

Give each child some modelling clay or play dough and ask them to make a model (or models) of some harvest produce. Provide them with tools to help make textures for their models. The models can be painted later in the session when the clay is dry (if your modelling clay hardens particularly quickly) or at home.

If you want to make your own play dough, the recipe on page 175 will enable you to supply large quantities cheaply.

PAINTING PLATES

 Time duration: 10 minutes

You will need: paper plates, paints, brushes.

Ask each child to paint a picture of their favourite food on the plate. You can use this activity later as the basis for prayers to thank God for all the good food he provides.

COOKING FOR HARVEST

BREAD PLAIT OR ROLL

 Time duration: 10 minutes

You will need: enough bread dough for the number of children (see recipe on page 177), baking parchment, hand-washing facilities, baking sheets, preheated hot oven, pencil.

If you have access to a bread machine, this can be useful for providing a ready supply of dough at the right time. If you have more children than can be catered for with one batch of bread machine dough, you can make the dough in advance. It will keep in a refrigerator for a couple of days, but you will need to bring it up to room temperature before the children use it. Children will need to wash their hands before they begin, and the tables and table coverings will need to be clean.

Give each child a quantity of dough (if they are making a plait, each child will need at least one quarter of a 650g batch of dough) and a sheet of baking parchment. Show them how to divide the dough into three equal amounts, roll them into long sausage shapes and make the plait. Younger children will need more help than older ones with this. If they are making rolls, they will need less dough, and should just knead the dough to get the feel of it and then shape it into rolls.

The plaits or rolls can be placed on small named sheets of baking parchment, left to rise in a warm place near the oven for 20–30 minutes and baked in the oven. Baking at about 200°C should take around 20 minutes, but this will depend on the size of the rolls, so keep an eye on them. If your church will be holding a Eucharist soon afterwards, they might make one roll especially for the service.

GAMES FOR HARVEST

BIBLE HARVEST MEMORY GAME

 Time duration: 10 minutes

You will need: a tray, cloth large enough to cover the tray, selection of food objects that are mentioned in the Bible, such as wheat, bread, grapes, wine, figs, mustard, yeast, flour, honey, milk, fish (don't use real fresh fish!), pomegranate and water.

Put a selection of items on a tray, let the children look at it for ten minutes or so and talk about each item. Talk to the children about Bible stories in which these items occur, or ask them if they can remember any stories that mention them. Cover the tray with a cloth and see how many items the children can remember. Older children can write them down. For younger ones, just asking them to say which ones they remember will be fine.

GUESS THE VEGETABLE

 Time duration: 15 minutes

You will need: feely boxes, a selection of vegetables with interesting textures (as many as you have feely boxes).

Using feely boxes for this activity is useful as it avoids using blindfolds, which are always a bit of a trial. Instructions for making a feely box are on page 181.

Place one fruit or vegetable inside each box and see if the children can guess what it is just by touch. Choose items with different textures and shapes, some more familiar than others—for example, orange, small Savoy cabbage, onion, celery, sweetcorn, walnuts in their shells.

DISCUSSION POINTS

These activities encourage the children to think of others and will work well to mark the start of any fundraising activity to help others in the Third World.

WATER ACTIVITY

 Time duration: 15 minutes

You will need: a large sheet of paper, a flip chart or whiteboard, pens, empty unbreakable containers.

This is an excellent way to help children to understand how thankful we should be for something as simple as water. Ask them where water comes from and how people living, say, 150 years ago would have got water (see if you can find out where the local wells were).

Trace the progress of our water by asking how it gets to the tap and tracing it back. Look also at where water goes when it runs back down the drain. Write up what happens on a flip chart or large piece of paper. You should end up with a diagram showing the lifecycle of water.

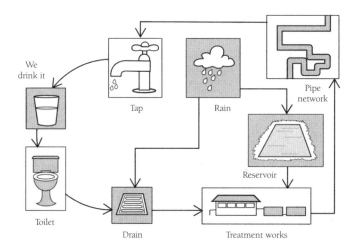

We drink it

Tap

Rain

Pipe network

Reservoir

Toilet

Drain

Treatment works

To finish off, talk about people who don't receive their water from a tap. Some people have to walk miles to fetch water, and even then it won't be very clean. Tell the children how, in some countries, people often carry water home on their heads. Get them to practise carrying unbreakable containers on their heads to see how easy it would be.

GEOGRAPHY ACTIVITY

Time duration: 15 minutes

You will need: a map of the world, a selection of food packets and tins with country of origin noted on the labels, coloured dot stickers.

This activity is designed to help the children realize that our food comes from all over the world. Show the children the map and check that they know where we live. Ask if they know any of the other countries. You might talk about different climates in different parts of the world.

Then ask each child to pick a food item (or one between two if you have a lot of children) and find where it comes from on the map. (Some children, particularly the younger ones, will need help with this.) Mark where the item comes from on the map with a coloured dot sticker. You could use this activity as the basis for prayers later.

For older children, finish off the discussion by sharing out some plastic toy food. Make sure you do this unfairly and arbitrarily, giving a lot more to a few children than to the rest. See what they think about this. See if they can then distribute it fairly without arguing about it.

PRAYERS FOR HARVEST

If you have used the idea for a discussion on where food comes from, you could use the food packets and/or the map for prayers.

If the children have painted plates with their favourite foods, you can use them as the basis for prayers. Perhaps the children could lay them on the altar as part of a thank you prayer.

Theme Ten

'LOVE CONQUERS FEAR'

A CHURCH-BASED ALTERNATIVE TO HALLOWE'EN

The celebration of Hallowe'en in the secular world is becoming increasingly popular, which provides an ideal opportunity to offer a church-based alternative to the usual activities.

'LOVE CONQUERS FEAR' BIBLE STORY

Romans 8:31–39 is an ideal passage to use for this workshop programme. If you memorize the passage and recite it to the children, this can have quite an impact. For the act of worship following the workshop, you could ask the children to help you with the reading by giving each of them a phrase to read in the right place.

If God is on our side, can anyone be against us? God did not keep back his own Son, but he gave him for us. If God did this, won't he freely give us everything else? If God says his chosen ones are acceptable to him, can anyone bring charges against them? Or can anyone condemn them? No indeed! Christ died and was raised to life, and now he is at God's right side, speaking to him for us. Can anything separate us from the love of Christ? Can trouble, suffering, and hard times, or hunger and nakedness, or danger and death? … In everything we have won more than a victory because of Christ who loves us. I am sure that nothing can separate us from God's love—

not life or death, not angels or spirits, not the present or the future, and not powers above or powers below. Nothing in all creation can separate us from God's love for us in Christ Jesus our Lord!
ROMANS 8:31–39

'LOVE CONQUERS FEAR' CRAFTS

FEAR PICTURES

 Time duration: 15 minutes

You will need: sheets of A4 paper (one per child), colouring materials, acetate sheets (one per child), glitter glue.

Give the children a piece of paper and ask them to draw and colour a picture of something they fear. When the pictures are ready, give everyone a sheet of acetate. Ask the children to write over the acetate (perhaps using glitter glue) the words 'Love conquers fear' in the shape of a crossword—with the 'o' and 'e' of 'conquers' standing as part of 'love' and 'fear'. Writing in glitter glue can be difficult, so for younger children you could either help them with it or provide pre-printed acetate sheets. They will need to use large letters so that the words fill the page.

Place the acetate over the scary picture they have produced and fix it down.

CHRISTIAN LANTERNS

 Time duration: 20 minutes

First, remove the labels from the bottles. Cut the top and base off each bottle, so that you have clear plastic cylinders. Have some pre-cut paper shapes depicting Christian symbols (for example, crosses, Pentecostal flames, crowns and so on). Use spray-on repositionable adhesive to make them tacky. Then get the children to arrange the shapes on the outsides of their lanterns and press them down.

They then need to cover the outsides of the tubes in acrylic paint, painting over the paper shapes. Before the paint is dry, but when it is no longer runny, peel off the paper shapes, leaving the clear plastic underneath. When the lanterns are placed over tealight candles the voids where the shapes were will let the light shine through clearly.

You could use the lanterns to decorate the church or have them lit during your service if you have one. Warnings about matches, candles and fire apply. If the children take the lanterns home, they and their parents should be issued with a sensible warning about fire: the lanterns will not be flame proof and can burn if candles are too close.

SAINTLY CROWNS

 Time duration: 10 minutes

You will need: pre-cut crown shapes made from metallic card for each child, glitter, sequins, holographic paper shapes, fake 'jewels' and so on, PVA glue, clear adhesive tape or stapler to secure the two ends of the crown.

Talk to the children about the fact that Hallowe'en is actually All Hallows' Eve, and the following day is the celebration for All Saints. In recognition, get the children to make crowns. Provide them with metallic card crown-shaped bases, and assorted 'jewels', tissue paper, foil, sweet wrappers, cellophane and so on to make their own saints' crowns. Fit the crown to the child's head when it is finished.

CROSSED MONSTERS

 Time duration: 15 minutes

You will need: sheets of A4 paper (one per child), wax crayons, watery water-based paint or ink, brushes.

Give each child a piece of A4 paper and ask them to draw large crosses in wax crayon all over the paper, or one large thick multi-coloured cross. They will need to press down quite hard. Then give them some thin water-based paint or ink (test the consistency in advance to make sure it is not too thick).

Ask the children to paint a monster over the top of the crosses: if the paint consistency is right, it won't work! You can then talk to them about how God is with us and if we trust in him we don't need to be afraid.

PLANTING BULBS

 Time duration: 10 minutes

You will need: spring bulbs, such as hyacinths, disposable gloves, compost, small plastic flower pots.

Now is a good time to plant bulbs for the spring. You will need to handle the bulbs carefully as some people have a reaction to them, so provide disposable gloves for the children to wear. As you are planting the bulbs, talk about how they seem dead, but there is the kernel of life inside. Whatever we fear, and however hopeless things seem, God is at work giving new life where there seems to be no hope.

MONSTER SKITTLES

 Time duration: 15–20 minutes

You will need: clean, empty and dry fizzy drinks cans (one per child), acrylic paint, pens, card, thin foam (optional), fast-drying glue, googly eyes (optional).

Prepare the cans in advance by putting some rice inside each one to give it a bit of weight, then gluing a circle of card over the top of the can. Paint each can and the card circle on top in bright colours using acrylic paint (you will probably need two coats) and let it dry thoroughly.

Let each child choose a can and ask them to decorate it to make it look like a really scary monster. They can do this using fast-drying paint, or pens, or by sticking on horns or teeth made of card or foam. Add googly eyes. For younger children you may need to have some pre-cut features for them to use, such as eyes, ears, claws, horns and so on. Older children would probably enjoy making their own decorations.

Use the cans as skittles in the game on page 134.

SPIDER WEB CAKE OR BISCUITS

 Time duration: 10 minutes

You will need: large ready-baked biscuits (one per child) or, if this is to be a group effort, one large ready-baked cake, coated with buttercream, glacé icing (icing sugar and water), food colouring, plastic or greaseproof bag with a small hole cut in one corner or spoons, cocktail sticks.

Show the children some pictures of spider webs covered in dew or frost, and talk about how wonderful and meticulous they are. Then invite each child to decorate a biscuit (or work together to decorate a large cake for everyone to share later) using ready-prepared bowls of glacé icing in different colours (including white).

To decorate the biscuits or cake, make a spiral shape on the surface by dribbling glacé icing out of a plastic or greaseproof bag with a small hole cut in one corner, or by using a small spoon. Then, with a cocktail stick, draw lines (not too deep) radiating from the centre. You should end up with a spider web effect.

'LOVE CONQUERS FEAR' GAMES

MONSTER SKITTLES

 Time duration: 15–20 minutes

You will need: monster skittles (see page 133), tennis ball, two small plastic flowerpots, two long garden canes.

Set up the skittles on the garden canes, balanced on flowerpots. If you have a lot of children attending, you may need more than one row, or, even better, divide them into groups to play. Give them a tennis ball and ask them to take turns trying to knock the monsters off the sticks.

Alternatively, make a bowling alley with the garden canes and flowerpots and set the skittles well spaced in rows at the end of the alley. Divide the children into teams and let each team member have one turn to roll the ball down the alley. Add up the score for each bowler. The winning team is the one with the highest number of skittles knocked down overall.

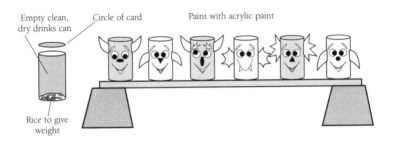

Empty clean, dry drinks can

Circle of card

Paint with acrylic paint

Rice to give weight

DISCUSSION ACTIVITIES

Talk about what we are most afraid of and why. You could use this to feed into the prayers.

'LOVE CONQUERS FEAR' PRAYERS

Consider a responsive prayer, using the children's own thoughts for the text of the prayer and then a response such as 'Lord, take away our fear'. Allowing the children to light a candle each would also be effective.

Theme 11

ALL SAINTS

This is a good time to explore the stories of people who have loved and had faith in God through the ages. The children will love to know that the word 'saint' was used in early Christian times to refer to ordinary Christians, so in fact the children themselves are 'saints'. When you choose which saints to concentrate on, try to ensure that you include some women and modern people.

Your church may be associated with a particular saint or you may have your very own picture or emblem of one in a stained-glass window. You might consider setting up an activity table for each saint and letting the children circulate around them as they wish.

STORIES FOR ALL SAINTS

The stories you tell will depend on the saints you explore in your activities. For this reason, in this session the stories linked with each saint are given with the related activities. Tell the stories as the children do the activities.

DISPLAYS FOR THE CHURCH

ST GEORGE COLLAGE

 Time duration: 10–15 minutes

You will need: a prepared collage board with St George and the dragon outlined on it, PVA glue, foil, green holographic paper circles, red metallic card, red and orange cellophane, painting or colouring materials, Post-it notes.

Have a pre-drawn outline of a dragon and St George already mounted on a collage board. Invite the children to fill in the St George figure with pieces of tin foil for his armour, then stick on circles cut from green holographic paper in an overlapping pattern for the dragon's scales. Make the dragon's eyes and tongue from the red metallic card and his fiery breath from red and orange cellophane.

Tell the children the story of St George while they work. We know very little about the real St George, but legend has it that he lived about 400 years or so after Jesus and he may have been a soldier. There are lots of popular legends about him in other countries as well as here. He is the patron saint (in other words, he watches over) England.

His story is that, once upon a time, a dragon arrived in a far-off country. Even its breath was poisonous. First it ate sheep, but when it ran out of them it started eating people. The local townsfolk had to offer it human victims to eat. They decided who should go by drawing lots. One day, the lot fell on the princess of the land. She had to go outside the town gates for the dragon to eat her up, but St George came to her rescue and defeated the dragon. The townsfolk were all so impressed that they were baptized as Christians.

We know this story isn't true because there are no such things as dragons, but even from stories that aren't strictly true we can learn something. There are lots of things that stop us from coming close to God. Some of them are difficult to get round or defeat, like the dragon, but with God's help, just like St George, we can do it.

Ask the children to write the names of some modern 'dragons' (such as war, poverty, selfishness, greed and so on) and stick them round the picture they have made.

CRAFTS FOR ALL SAINTS

ST CECILIA INSTRUMENTS

 Time duration: 10 minutes

You will need: boxes, greaseproof paper, elastic bands, paper, paper cups for shakers, 'beans', sticky tape, pencils.

As St Cecilia is the patron saint of music, ask the children to make musical instruments. For example, use paper cups and beans to make shakers, boxes and greaseproof paper for drums, boxes and rubber bands for 'guitars'. You might use these instruments to help perform a song later—perhaps 'When the saints go marching in'.

Talk about St Cecilia. We know very little about her life, but she is celebrated for being the patron saint of music—so that's why we're making musical instruments. We think that she lived in Italy about 200 or 300 years after Jesus. She was brought up in a Christian household and had a very strong Christian faith. When she married, she insisted that her husband converted to the Christian faith. When he did this, he and she were killed because of their Christian faith. A church was built on the site of the house in Rome where she had lived and, eventually, she was adopted as the patron saint of music, first in Italy and then in England. Her festival day is 22 November.

ST PETER KEY PICTURES

 Time duration: 10–15 minutes

You will need: ready-cut key stencils, stencil brushes or sponges, bright paints (perhaps fluorescent and/or luminous), black sugar paper.

St Peter's symbol is a key and he is often pictured holding the key of heaven. Give each child a sheet of black paper and some pre-cut stencils of keys in different shapes and sizes. Ask the children to make pictures using the stencils. You will need to watch that they don't overload their brushes: stencil painting is best done with the brushes or sponges almost dry.

While the children are doing this, talk to them about St Peter. He was one of Jesus' disciples and a fisherman. He also became the leader among the other disciples after the Holy Spirit came at Pentecost. Jesus called Peter a 'rock' on whom the Church would be built (Matthew 16:13–19). Peter was one of Jesus' closest friends. He witnessed the transfiguration and he was with Jesus when he prayed in the garden of Gethsemane. He followed Jesus to the place where he was held after he was arrested, but then denied that he knew him.

In the Bible, Peter comes across as very much like you and me, and often asks the questions we want to ask. He was the disciple who tried to walk across the water to meet Jesus and he was very impetuous. In church tradition he is seen holding the keys to heaven. His emblem shows an upside-down cross (he was eventually crucified for being a Christian, but he asked to be crucified upside down because he thought he wasn't worthy to die in the same way as Jesus). His emblem also depicts crossed keys to represent the keys of heaven.

ST STEPHEN STONES

 Time duration: 10 minutes

You will need: clean dry large stones or cobbles (obtainable from garden centres), paint, brushes.

St Stephen was the Church's first martyr. He was stoned to death because he would not give up his Christian faith. Give each child a stone and some paint and ask them to paint crosses on the stones. You could show them pictures of different types of cross, so they can choose which ones to paint.

Tell the children about St Stephen. A martyr is someone who would rather die than say they don't love God. St Stephen was a very brave man and had to do just that. He was a Jew who had believed that Jesus was the Son of God. After Jesus' death and resurrection, Stephen kept teaching people about Jesus. His insistence that Jesus had risen from the dead annoyed the Jewish authorities. Stephen told them that Jesus was the saviour the Jews had been waiting for and that they should not have killed him. The Jewish authorities were so angry that they arranged for Stephen to be killed by stoning him to death: a crowd of people threw stones at him until he died. He died very bravely, still worshipping God and praying for forgiveness for his persecutors (Acts 7:54–60).

ST AUGUSTINE MITRES

 Time duration: 10 minutes

You will need: card mitre shapes, PVA glue, glitter, shiny pens, sticky tape.

The children are unlikely to have heard of St Augustine, so you will need to explain that he was the first Archbishop of Canterbury. Ask the children to make and decorate mitres. Provide pre-cut mitre shapes (two for each child), with some tabs or a band to attach them round each child's head.

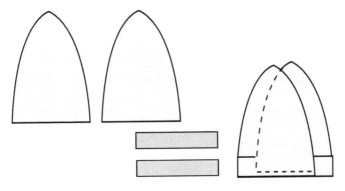

Talk about St Augustine. Does anyone know who the most senior priest in the Church of England is? At the time of writing, his name is Dr Rowan Williams and the position he holds is Archbishop of Canterbury. There have been many other Archbishops of Canterbury before him; but the first one was St Augustine.

St Augustine was sent to England from Rome by a pope called Gregory. Gregory had wanted to send someone to England for some time to teach the English people about God and Jesus, and he chose Augustine to do this work. Augustine didn't really want to go because he was frightened about going to a strange land, but Gregory persuaded him and he went. When he and his friends came to England, it wasn't as bad as they had feared and the local king (Ethelbert) welcomed them and gave them somewhere to live.

St Augustine travelled around, teaching people. The king was so impressed with Augustine that he wanted to be a Christian, and he was baptized. Lots of his subjects were baptized, too. They started to build a cathedral at Canterbury and that's where the English church started to grow.

GLADYS AYLWARD LANTERNS

 Time duration: 10–15 minutes

You will need: black paper, shiny or holographic paper, scissors, glue sticks, stapler or sticky tape.

Gladys Aylward is a modern saint who rescued children from China. Get the children to make Chinese lanterns as a celebration of her life. Each child will need a sheet of black paper folded in half. Cut slits in the paper as shown in the diagram. Open the paper out and fold round to make into cylinders. Insert a cylinder of coloured holographic paper for the light. Add a paper loop for a handle.

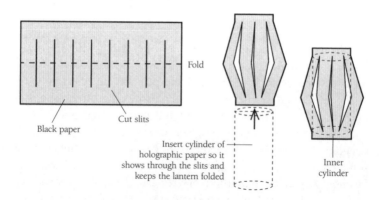

Black paper

Cut slits

Fold

Insert cylinder of holographic paper so it shows through the slits and keeps the lantern folded

Inner cylinder

Tell the children about Gladys Aylward. She was born in London in 1902. She was a missionary and was convinced that God wanted her to go to China to teach people about God. It took her a while to save up the money, but at last she had enough to be able to buy a ticket to China. She lived there for many years and taught the people. She and another woman opened an inn where travellers could rest and hear stories about Jesus.

In those days, it was a custom in China for baby girls to have their feet wrapped up in bandages (the people thought small feet were more beautiful). Wrapping babies' feet up to stop them growing meant that when the girls grew they couldn't walk properly. Gladys was chosen to inspect the feet of Chinese baby girls and save them from this cruel practice.

One day, a war broke out between the Chinese and the Japanese, which meant that the area where Gladys lived became very dangerous and she had to leave. Instead of just leaving all the people behind, she took more than 100 Chinese children with her across the mountains and over a great river so that they would be safe.

ST MARY HYACINTHS

 Time duration: 10–15 minutes

You will need: small plastic flower pots (one per child), compost, hyacinth bulbs (one per child), Disposable gloves.

Hyacinths are often associated with Mary, so give each child a flowerpot, some compost and a hyacinth bulb. You will also need to provide latex gloves, as hyacinth bulbs can cause a reaction on some people's hands.

While the children are planting their bulbs, tell them about Mary. She was the mother of Jesus. She was just an ordinary girl, but God had chosen her for a very special job. One day an angel came to see Mary. The angel said she would have a baby and explained that he would be God's Son. God would do great things through him.

How do you think Mary felt? Scared? I should think anyone would be very frightened! But Mary was brave. She understood that having a baby when you were not yet married, in those days, was likely to cause lots of people to be unkind to her. But because God asked her, she said 'yes'. When Jesus was born, Mary held all the special things that were said about him in her heart.

When Jesus was twelve, she was very worried when he got lost in the temple in Jerusalem. Mary and Joseph had travelled to Jerusalem from their home in Nazareth to visit the temple and, on their way home, they discovered that Jesus was missing. Imagine his mother's worry as she ran from place to place searching for him, until she eventually found him, safe and unconcerned, sitting in the temple listening and speaking with the priests.

Mary was present when Jesus performed his first miracle by turning water into wine at the wedding in Cana. She was also present at his death and witnessed her son being crucified. She had known right from the very beginning how special he was, but it must have broken her heart to have seen him so cruelly put to death.

DISCUSSION ACTIVITIES

ST PAUL LETTERS

 Time duration: 10–15 minutes

You will need: paper, pens, pencils, crayons, Bible.

St Paul was a great letter writer; much of the New Testament was written by him. Tell the children about all the letters he wrote to other Christians while he was travelling around telling people about Jesus, and point out where they are in the Bible.

Invite the children to write a letter to the PCC (or your governing council) about how the children see church—perhaps how it could be better for them. If the children are very young, get them to draw pictures instead. It is important that they are delivered to the PCC and that the children receive a response.

Talk to the children about St Paul. They may not be very familiar with him, but St Paul is a really 'big' saint in the church. How do you think his story starts? Actually he was one of Jesus' biggest enemies. In those days, his name was not Paul, but Saul. He was a Jewish leader who was very active in persecuting the early Christians. He was present when St Stephen was stoned to death. He wanted to wipe out everyone who believed in Jesus. One day, Saul set off on a journey to a town called Damascus to arrest the Christians who lived there. But on the way he saw a blinding flash of light from the sky and he heard Jesus asking why he was persecuting the Christians. When that happened he suddenly found that he was completely blind. His fellow travellers had to help him to get to the next town. While he was there, God sent someone to heal his blindness.

After that, Saul changed his name to Paul and began to follow Jesus. Jesus led him on many long journeys. This time, instead of arresting the Christians, he visited them and encouraged them in their faith. It was because of St Paul that many of the early churches were formed. Because he was travelling a lot of the time, he kept in touch with the Christians he had visited by writing letters to them. Today, we too can read some of these letters in the Bible.

PRAYERS FOR ALL SAINTS

ST MARY MAGDALENE PRAYER CHAIN

 Time duration: 10–15 minutes

You will need: pre-cut strips cut from brightly coloured paper, pre-cut strips cut from gold or silver holographic paper, stapler, glue sticks.

St Mary Magdalene was one of Jesus' special friends, so a friendship paper chain would be a good activity to celebrate her. Have lots of pre-cut paper chain links. Give each person three links and ask them to write their own name on one and the name of a friend on each of the others. Link the three pieces together, either by gluing or by stapling (with the help of an adult). When all the sets of three links are assembled, join them all together using the additional links cut from silver or gold paper to represent Jesus linking us all together in friendship. Use the friendship chain as the basis for prayers about unity and friendship.

Tell the children about Mary Magdalene. Mary Magdalene was one of Jesus' best friends. She was someone for whom lots of things had gone wrong in her life, but when she met Jesus her life changed and she started to follow him and live as God wanted. She was the first person to see Jesus on the first Easter morning when he had risen from the dead (Luke 8:1–3; John 20:1–18).

SUMMER HOLIDAY CLUB THEME: JOURNEYS

These workshop plans are presented as a series that would be suitable for a five-day holiday club. However, they were conceived and tested as individual sessions, so they will work either way.

Sometimes, particularly during the long summer season of ordinary time, themes for your workshops might not be obvious from the point of view of the Christian year. This is an opportunity to enjoy telling the children Bible stories that they might not otherwise hear, especially some of the Old Testament stories.

The theme of journeys fits well with the end of the school year when many of the children might be travelling to go on holiday. There are plenty of journeys in the Bible to tell the children about.

SESSION 1: NOAH'S JOURNEY

STORIES FOR NOAH'S JOURNEY

You will find the story of Noah in Genesis 6:1—9:17. The story can be told using the *Godly Play* approach (see resources on page 189 for details). There are also many pictures books telling the story, or you could try an audience participation version, giving the children actions or responses to go along with the story.

DISPLAYS FOR THE CHURCH

Noah's ark display

 Time duration: 20 minutes (pre-session preparation)

You will need: a large piece of cardboard or a section cut from a cardboard box, paint and brushes, animals made by the children.

Before the session, make a backdrop against which to display cardboard tube animals (see the craft activity on page 151). If you have time, you could make the backdrop as an activity with the children.

SONGS FOR NOAH'S JOURNEY

There are lots of good songs about Noah that the children could learn and sing later to their parents and/or the congregation., such as 'Rise and Shine'. (See the Song Books list on page 188 for ideas.)

CRAFTS FOR NOAH'S JOURNEY

Cork boats

 Time duration: 15 minutes

You will need: corks (four per child), plastic drinking straws, paper, pens, large seed tray (or similar) for water, at least 75cm square, water, strong glue, Plasticine.

This is a good activity for summer when there is a chance that the children could test their boats outside (if it is raining, you can always use the tray of water inside). Before the session, lay down four corks, side by side, and glue them together to form a flat raft. Use two dots of glue for each join, leaving a gap between the dots. A hot glue gun will do the trick, although you will need to make sure the cork surfaces are grease-free so that the glue will stick. Cut the paper to size to make the sails.

Give each child a pre-glued cork raft and a straw. They will need to flatten one end of the straw and push it between the two middle corks of their raft and then use a piece of Plasticine to help keep it in place and add stability underneath the raft.

Cut two slits in the piece of paper sail so that it can be slid over the mast. Get each child to write their name, or otherwise decorate the sail, so that they can identify their raft. Thread the sail on to the mast.

The boats can now be tested. Put them into the dry seed tray, add water and watch the boats rising and floating on the flood. The children will be able to propel the boats across the water by blowing on the sails.

Rainbow mobiles

 Time duration: 15 minutes

You will need: white card, gold card, silver card, pair of compasses, scissors, pens, glue or sticky tape, acetate or thread.

This activity involves preparing a lot of pre-cut shapes, unless you are doing this with older children (and with enough time) for them to do their own cutting. You will need to prepare one pre-cut rainbow shape for each child. To do this, draw circles on the white card with the pair of compasses and then cut them in half, so that each circle yields two rainbows. Next, cut out sun shapes from the gold card (one for each child) and raindrop shapes from the silver card (seven for each child).

You can use thread to suspend the items from the rainbow, but you may find it quicker to pre-cut strips of acetate and use these to suspend the shapes. The acetate can be folded so that the raindrops seem to spray out.

Ask each child to colour in the rainbow shape in rainbow colours. If they want to follow the exact colours of the rainbow, you will probably need to remind them what they are and what order they come in (red, orange, yellow, green, blue, indigo, violet). Use sticky tape or glue dots to attach an acetate strip to both the rainbow shape and the sun on one side and the raindrops on the other.

While you're doing this activity, talk to the children about God's promise as represented by the rainbow. You might also like to tell them how rainbows appear when sunshine and rain are mixed together, and that there is always a rainbow somewhere on earth, so God's sign can be seen somewhere on our planet at all times. When rainbows are photographed from space, you can see that they are actually circular, without beginning or end.

BASED ON AN IDEA FROM *HERE'S ONE I MADE EARLIER* BY KATHRYN COPSEY, (SCRIPTURE UNION, 1995).

Chalk pavement art

 Time duration: 15 minutes

You will need: coloured and white chalks, a paved path, black sugar paper (in case of rain).

Before undertaking this activity, make sure you have the approval of your churchwarden or whoever is in charge of the path you have chosen on which to indulge in some pavement art!

Invite the children to draw pictures to illustrate creation in chalk on the path. Take photographs of their work, but remind them that when the rain comes (as it surely will) it will wash their pictures away just like the flood washed all of Noah's world away. When the water had gone, he wouldn't have recognized anything—no houses or villages or living things except what had been on the ark.

If it is raining, the children can do their pictures inside on black paper instead, but show them how easily chalk is brushed off.

Cardboard tube animals

 Time duration: 15 minutes

You will need: cardboard tubes (two per child), paint and brushes, glue, card, collage items such as paper, tissue paper, feathers, leather and so on, googly eyes.

Prepare the cardboard tubes as described on page 90. Give each child a pair of tubes, so they can make a pair of animals. Have a good supply of paint, card, collage items and googly eyes so that each child can turn their tube into the animal of their choice. If you have a prepared an ark scene, the animals can be displayed as part of that, or the children can take them home.

Animal masks

 Time duration: 15 minutes

You will need: card cut into basic mask shapes, collage materials to decorate, such as paper, tissue paper, wool, feathers, leather, cotton wool, thin coloured foam and so on, glue, paint and brushes, elastic, stapler, sticky tape.

Invite each child to decorate their mask to make an animal face. When they've finished, staple the elastic to fit the child's head, making sure the staples' points are facing out. Cover the staples with sticky tape to prevent them from causing discomfort. You could use the masks at the end of the session to recap the story of Noah's ark.

Rainbow doves

 Time duration: 15 minutes

You will need: white card cut into dove shapes, rainbow-coloured paper cut to size, pens.

Cut out the dove shapes and then cut a slot in the side of each one. Give each child a sheet of rainbow-coloured paper. Get them to fold the paper up in a concertina so that it is no wider than the slot. Feed the paper through the slot cut in the side of the dove and then open up the concertinas on both sides of the dove to make the wings.

The children could decorate their doves with feathers or by writing a message or drawing a picture about what the story of Noah means to them.

GAMES FOR NOAH'S JOURNEY

Racing cork boats

If the children have made cork boats, they will enjoy racing them on the tray of water. This will do just as well as a pool or pond, if not better and somewhat safer, as the tray will prevent the need for anyone to wade in to rescue lost vessels.

STORIES FOR THE EXODUS

The story of the exodus is a long one. Instead of hearing everything at one sitting, you might consider breaking the story into three sections (the exodus, wandering in the desert and the Ten Commandments and, finally, entering the promised land) to be told at intervals during the afternoon. *Godly Play* works well for these stories (see page 189 for resources). You could also use any of the stories from the time when the Israelites were wandering in the wilderness, if you wanted to.

DISPLAYS FOR THE CHURCH

Road signs

 Time duration: 15 minutes

You will need: large circles and round-cornered triangles cut from red card, the same shapes but made smaller cut from white card, black paper, scissors, glue, long cardboard tubes (optional).

Talk to the children about how the Bible can show us the way to live well. Then show them a copy of the Highway Code, especially the page with road signs, and invite them to make up some road signs by cutting and sticking shapes from the black paper on to the white triangles or circles to show people how to live well (as opposed to drive well). The white card can then be mounted on the red to give a road sign effect.

These signs could be fixed on cardboard tubes (such as the insides of wrapping paper) and mounted on chairs or the ends of pews for display in church.

Compasses

 Time duration: 10 minutes

You will need: thick white card cut into circles with the centre marked, split-pin paper fasteners, compass 'needles' cut from thick white card, pens, map, a real compass.

Show the children what a compass looks like and how it works by always showing you where north is. Also show them some maps and point out that north is marked on them, too. Then give the children a pre-cut circle each and ask them to decorate them to create their compass. They may need help in marking the points of the compass. Give them each a compass 'needle', also cut from card, to decorate. Fix the 'needle' to the compass base with a paper fastener.

You might like to talk to the children about what things we can use to find our way on our spiritual journey: the Bible can be a bit like a map and compass showing us the way to God.

Packed suitcases

 Time duration: 10 minutes

You will need: thin card, pictures cut from magazines, glue, scissors.

To prepare the 'suitcases', fold a thin piece of card in half and cut out a suitcase shape so that the hinge edge is along the folded edge of the card. When you open up the 'suitcase' you have a double shape. Give one of these to each child. Ask them to pack their suitcase by choosing from the magazine pictures items that they will need on their journey. Talk about what we do and don't need and what God provides us with.

Personal arks

 Time duration: 15 minutes

You will need: small gold boxes (obtainable from craft shops, or on the Internet), small copies of the Ten Commandments, glue, sequins, beads and so on, glitter glue, narrow ribbon.

Give each child a small gold box and a selection of sequins, glitter glue and any other (small) shiny things and ask them to decorate their boxes so that they look really special. Talk to them about how the Israelites made the ark of the covenant to carry the Ten Commandments with them as they travelled. When the boxes are finished, put a copy of the Ten Commandments (paraphrased from Exodus 20:3–17) into each box and tie them up with pretty ribbon.

GAMES FOR THE EXODUS

Memory game

 Time duration: 10 minutes

You will need: a tray, a cloth large enough to cover the tray, journey-related items such as a map, compass, guidebook, shoe, Bible, Highway Code, bottle of water, torch and so on.

Put the items on a tray and let the children look at them carefully. Talk about why each one is necessary, then cover them with a cloth and see how many the children can remember.

SESSION 3: JONAH'S JOURNEY

STORIES FOR JONAH'S JOURNEY

The book of Jonah is very short, making it easy to learn and retell to the children, but there are also lots of picture-book variations on the market. The story is dramatic and works well told to the children in your own words if you have the confidence to do this.

DISPLAYS FOR THE CHURCH

Box scenes

 Time duration: 30 minutes

You will need: large heavy-duty cardboard boxes, emulsion paint and brush, collage items (sandpaper, foil, crêpe paper, card, coloured paper, small boxes and tubes, metallic paper and so on), paint (optional), glue, thread, paper to make labels.

Making scenery in boxes is always a popular activity and works well for children in small groups or even in pairs. To prepare the boxes, first tape them up so there are no loose flaps, then cut them open carefully (see diagram) so that one box forms the basis for two sets of scenery. Have as many boxes as you can think of scenes for (such as space, ocean, glacier, desert, forest, city, village, countryside, industrial landscape), as God is with us in each of these.

When you cut the boxes, you may find that odd flaps of card fall out, but these are easy to glue back into place. Once the glue is dry, paint the boxes inside with at least two coats of ordinary white emulsion to give a good basis for the collage work.

Provide a selection of collage materials (and paint if desired) and

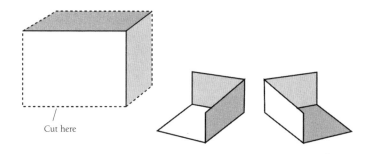

Cut here

ask the children to create whichever scene is required. Labels made from laminated paper are a nice touch when the boxes are ready to go on display. Perhaps they could read something like 'God is with is in the desert; God is with us in space; God is with us in...' and so on. Use these as a starting point to talk about how God is with us wherever we go.

CRAFTS FOR JONAH'S JOURNEY

Lolly-stick photo frames

> ⏰ **Time duration: 10 minutes**
>
> **You will need:** lolly sticks (available from craft shops) painted in bright colours (eight per child), glue, digital camera and means of printing pictures.

You will need to have the consent of parents or carers to take the photographs for this activity. Before the session, practise taking and printing pictures to make sure you can print them out at the correct size for the frames and to see how much they will need to be trimmed. The printing for the pictures can be done at someone's home nearby if necessary.

As each child arrives, take a photograph of him or her with a digital camera. (You need to be quite sure that you have a photograph of everyone or there'll be tears!) While the pictures are being printed, the children can be getting on with another activity. When the photographs are ready, the children can make frames for their own photograph.

Lay the lolly sticks on top of the picture to form a frame, with two lolly sticks lying parallel on each side. Glue the sticks together where they overlap at the corners. You can then trim the picture and glue it to the back of the frame. Write a suitable message round the outside of the frame such as 'God is with me'.

Junk modelling

 Time duration: 30 minutes

You will need: junk boxes, cartons and paper, glue (PVA, glue dots, glue gun, glue sticks), double-sided sticky tape, paint and brushes.

Invite the children to use the 'junk' and glue to make models of means of transport—cars, buses, trains, spaceships, boats or anything they like. They can paint the models either at home or at a subsequent session or, if you have really fast-drying glue, later on during the same session.

If the glossy finish on some cartons means that poster paint won't stick, you could try acrylic paint instead, or mix some flour in with the paint.

'Aeronautical engineering'

⏰ **Time duration:** 10 minutes

You will need: sheets of A4 paper.

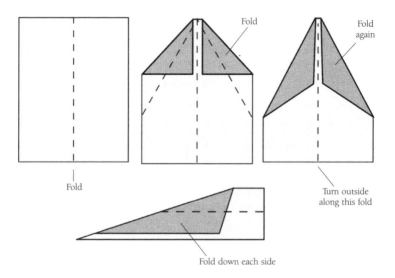

Fold

Fold

Fold again

Turn outside along this fold

Fold down each side

Making and testing paper aeroplanes is great fun and ideal for a church situation if it is raining, as naves usually give a nice long flight path! Try testing different designs to see which flies the best. If you can't remember how to fold a standard paper plane, there's a diagram below. You could then turn the activity into a game to see whose plane will fly the furthest.

STORIES FOR PAUL'S JOURNEY

You will probably need to talk broadly about who Paul was and why he is famous. There are a number of stories about him that will catch the children's imaginations, such as the story of his conversion on the road to Damascus, the story of Paul's and Silas' release from prison and the conversion of the guard, the story of the shipwreck and the viper on the island of Malta. If you are able to, memorize the stories and just tell them to the children. This is quite dramatic and should keep them in their seats.

DISPLAYS FOR THE CHURCH

Plotting Paul's journeys

 Time duration: 15 minutes

You will need: a large copy of a Bible map of the eastern Mediterranean (preferably with biblical names marked on it), coloured self-adhesive dots.

Tell the children about Paul's journeys. Ask them to find the places he went to and mark them with the coloured dots on the map to show the journeys. Use different coloured dots for each journey. Here is a summary of his travels.

Paul travelled all round the eastern part of the Mediterranean, telling people about Jesus and founding churches in many different places. A large portion of the New Testament comprises letters he wrote to Christians in these places. The letters are known in the Bible either by the name of the person he was writing to (such as Timothy or Philemon) or by the places where they lived (such as the Ephesians, who were the people of Ephesus).

Travelling took a long time in those days because there were no cars or trains or planes. People walked or rode a horse or donkey, or went by boat, so getting anywhere took a long time.

I've got a map here and we're going to work out where Paul travelled.

His first journey started at Antioch in Syria. Paul crossed the sea to Salamis on the island of Cyprus, then to Paphos on the other side of the island. Then he crossed the sea again and travelled to Antioch of Pisidia, then on to Lystra, and Derbe, then back to Lystra, and Antioch of Pisidia, on to Attalia and then he sailed back to Antioch in Syria.

The second journey started in Antioch in Syria. Paul travelled to Tarsus, Derbe, Lystra, Antioch of Pisidia, Philippi, Thessalonica, Athens, Corinth, over the sea to Ephesus, by sea again to Caesarea, then Jerusalem and back to Antioch in Syria.

The third journey started again in Antioch in Syria. Paul started as before by going to Tarsus, Derbe, Lystra and Antioch of Pisidia. Then he travelled to Ephesus, round the coast, past Athens, back to Corinth, up to Thessalonica, then Philippi and back by sea to Tyre, down to Jerusalem and then Caesarea.

The fourth and final journey started in Caesarea. Paul journeyed to Tyre, then he went by sea to Crete, then Malta, up to Syracuse in Sicily and on by sea to Rome where eventually he was put to death by the Romans.

CRAFTS FOR PAUL'S JOURNEY

Jointed snakes

 Time duration: 15 minutes

You will need: thin coloured card, 30/60 set square, split-pin paper fasteners, hole punch, googly eyes, thin red ribbon, metallic pens, glue sticks, scissors.

Cut a series of identical diamond shapes from some thin card using a ruler and set square. Punch holes near the two wider angles. Get the children to decorate each segment of their snake with metallic pens. The two points of each segment can then be glued together to form a tube. Use split-pin paper fasteners to attach them together to make a snake that twists and turns. Use the thin red ribbon to make a flickering tongue, stick googly eyes on to the head end and shape the tail to a point.

FROM *FUN TO MAKE* BY GILLIAN SOUTER (OFF THE SHELF PUBLISHING, 2001)

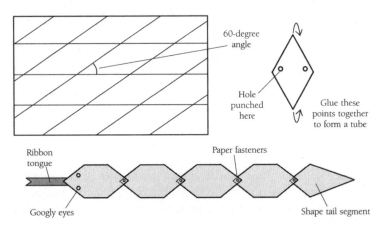

Paper chains

 Time duration: 10 minutes

You will need: strips of coloured paper, glue, stapler (optional).

Make paper chains in the usual way with strips of paper and glue or a stapler (for fast, strong joins). You could fasten everyone's short chain together to make a long one and use it to decorate your church. This activity will fit well with the story of Paul's imprisonment.

Prison pictures

 Time duration: 15 minutes

You will need: sheets of A4 paper, paint and brushes, black card, scissors, glue sticks or dots.

Give each child a piece of paper and ask them to paint a picture of 'freedom': how freedom would feel, what it might look like or a place where the children might feel free. Then have some black card ready cut to form a frame for the picture and bars across it. Mount the freedom picture behind the bars.

Postcards

 Time duration: 10 minutes

You will need: plain blank postcards, pens, crayons or pencils.

Get the children to design and write a postcard. They could either leave them in church on display or take them away and send them. If you wished, they could draw a picture of something they have learned in church that day and, in the writing, tell a friend about it. Alternatively, they could imagine the sort of postcards that Paul might have sent from one of his journeys or from prison.

Passports

 Time duration: 15 minutes

You will need: thick A5 paper folded to make booklets, photograph from digital camera (another print from the activity on page 157 or a fresh picture), pens, pencils, stamps and inkpads, a real passport.

Show the children a passport and explain what it is for. Show them the photograph and description and the stamps showing where the passport holder has travelled into and out of various countries.

Give each child two or three sheets of folded A5 paper and invite them to make their own passports. You will need a digital photograph of each child, which could be taken and printed out at the beginning of the session (with parental permission for the taking of the picture). Stick the photographs in the 'passports' and ask each child to add their names and other details. They can then decorate the pages using the stamps and inkpads.

GAMES FOR PAUL'S JOURNEY

Snakes and ladders

 Time duration: 20 minutes

You will need: snakes and ladders boards (one per group of four children), counters (one per child), dice (one per board).

To tie in with the story of the viper on Malta, play a game of snakes and ladders. Split the children into groups of four and give each group a board and a dice. Give each child a counter.

Get the children all to start their games at the same time, so that you have an overall winner as well as a winner in each group. Sweet vipers would make suitable prizes for the winners, but check food allergies before giving the sweets.

Travelling in biblical times

 Time duration: 15–20 minutes

You will need: sheets of A4 paper, pens and/or pencils.

If you have plotted Paul's journeys on a large map, this will make a good starting point for a discussion about the difficulties involved in making journeys in those days and what an achievement it was for Paul to have travelled so widely.

Talk about how Paul wrote lots of letters to the places he had visited, where he had founded churches. Find these places on the map. Suggest that the children write letters to the PCC (or your church's governing body). If the children are not old enough to write a letter, just a sentence or a drawing will be fine. They might write something about the Bible or about what they have learned in these sessions. If you do this, though, please make sure that a response is sent back to the children.

STORIES FOR THE CHRISTIAN JOURNEY

After all the stories about biblical characters in the previous workshops, a passage about the Christian life from one of Paul's letters is an appropriate way to end the series. There are many to choose from, but Ephesians 3:14–21 would set the scene well and provide a positive conclusion to the programme.

DISPLAYS FOR THE CHURCH

Christian journey collage

 Time duration: 25 minutes

You will need: a prepared collage board, collage items (paper, card, foam, magazine pictures, foil, fabric, leather, feathers, shiny materials and so on), glue.

Prepare a board for your collage. Get the children to decide what items they will need for the Christian journey. To help them in their thinking, start by asking how we know we're going in the right direction if we are on a journey to, for example, school, the shops or the swimming pool. Lead on from this to talk about how we find the way God wants us to go on our Christian journey. We will need a Bible for a map, prayer to ask for directions, fellowship with other Christians for companionship and mutual support, Jesus the light of the world as a torch, Jesus the bread of life for food, the water of baptism to keep us clean and so on.

Spend some time working out how these things will be depicted. You may need labels to make clear exactly what the display is about. You could use pictures the children have done for each item, a collage made from magazine pictures or a mixture of the two. When the children have completed their work, read Ephesians 3:14–21 as a reflection on what they have done.

Footprints painting

 Time duration: 25 minutes

You will need: lining wallpaper, poster paint, brushes, bowls, water, soap, towels to wash feet, polythene dustsheets.

A footprint painting can be displayed in church as a frieze with a suitable caption or used as a background for the Christian journey collage above. Spread the lining paper on the floor, with polythene dustsheets underneath to protect the floor. Paint the soles of each child's feet and get them to walk down the length of the paper. Use lots of different colours to create an interesting effect.

CRAFTS FOR THE CHRISTIAN JOURNEY

Footprints Bible verses

 Time duration: 15 minutes

You will need: sheets of A4 paper, poster paint, brushes, foot-washing equipment as above, foot-shaped print blocks (optional).

Give each child a sheet of paper and either get them to do prints of their own feet or give them small foot-shaped print blocks to create a picture. The print blocks are made by cutting foot shapes from some craft foam, gluing them to corrugated card and trimming round the edge. Add handles to the block and then apply paint (sparingly).

Have spare sheets of paper to hand, so the children can get the hang of the technique before doing their pictures. Add a Bible verse, choosing either a verse from Ephesians 3:14–21 (such as 'Stand firm and be deeply rooted in Christ's love') or ask the children to add a Bible verse of their choice (perhaps a memory verse or a verse from a well-known song).

COOKING FOR THE CHRISTIAN JOURNEY

Food for the journey

 Time duration: 20 minutes

You will need: sliced bread, butter or spread, a selection of sandwich fillings.

This would be a good way to round off the holiday club as a final activity, but make sure you have plenty of time for it. Talk about what food you might take with you. Invite the children to help you make some sandwiches, then go for a short walk to a place where there is some grass for the children to sit on. Enjoy the picnic: take some juice and biscuits, too. Picnic inside if it is raining.

GAMES FOR THE CHRISTIAN JOURNEY

As this is the final workshop in the series, some party games would be appropriate. Use games you know the children enjoy, or you might include some of the ideas below.

Guess the place

Tailor the places you use to the ages of the children who will be playing. If the children are young, use the names of places in your locality. You might even make it as simple as 'school', 'shop', 'swings' and so on. Use local towns for slightly older children and different countries for the oldest ones.

To play the game, whisper a location to one child. The others have to guess where that place is by asking questions to which the child with the card can answer only 'yes' or 'no'. Put a limit on the number of questions asked. If the location is not guessed within this limit, put the card to the back of the pile and choose another location and another child.

Mode of transport

Put the children into three or four groups, with an equal number of children in each group. Set the groups apart from each other. Sit in the middle of the room. Get one child from each group to come up to you to collect a card, return to their group and mime the mode of transport on the card to the rest of the group. Once the group has guessed the mime, the next person in the group goes up for a card and so on until all the cards for that group have been used up. The winning group is the one that guesses all the modes of transport first. Ideas might include flying, walking, driving, sailing, cycling, horseriding, motorbiking, using a submarine and so on.

Guess who?

 Time duration: 10 minutes

You will need: items of clothing or objects to provide hints.

Recap the holiday club by testing the children on the people they have learned about in the past week. Get a grown-up helper to dress up or bring an object associated with one of the biblical characters from the previous four workshops, and see if the children know who is being represented.

Directions game

Put the children in pairs. Tell one child in each pair that they need to conduct their partner to a place, but they mustn't tell the partner where the place is. Instead they must give them directions on how to get there: for example, 'turn to your right and take ten paces' and so on. Once the partner has reached the destination, let the children swap roles and give them another destination.

DISCUSSION ACTIVITIES

Where are we going on holiday?

 Time duration: 10 minutes

You will need: a map of the world or the country where you live, self-adhesive coloured dots.

Have a map of the world on which to mark where the children are going on holiday. Talk about what the children know about these places and how people might live in these countries. If you are unlikely to have many children going on holidays abroad, have a map of your own country. Use the activity as a starter for prayers about the places we will be visiting on holiday, and lead this in to prayers for when you will all be coming together again after the holidays.

PRAYERS FOR THE CHRISTIAN JOURNEY

Praying for others

Use the above activity as a starting point for prayers. Pray for people who live in the places we will visit and for all travellers to and from those places. Pray for the places that we don't want to visit on holiday because of drought, famine, war or oppression.

APPENDICES

SAMPLE WORKSHOP PLAN

(FOR ADVENT)

Workshop plans for all sessions, with suggested age bandings, can be found on the website: www.barnabasinchurches.org.uk.

PARABLES OF THE KINGDOM

MATTHEW 13:31–32, 33, 44, 45–46

Plan 1 (children aged 3–8)

TIME	ACTIVITY	DETAILS
10 minutes	Registration	Pen, paper, registration forms, badges and blanks
10 minutes	Story	The story of the mustard seed
10 minutes	Craft (3 rotating groups)	Crowns
10 minutes	Craft (3 rotating groups)	Heart cards
10 minutes	Game (3 rotating groups)	Treasure hunt
10 minutes	Story	The story of the yeast
10 minutes	Break	Refreshments
10 minutes	Story	The story of the valuable pearl
10 minutes	Church display (3 rotating groups)	'The kingdom of heaven is like...' pictures
10 minutes	Craft (3 rotating groups)	Mustard and cress
10 minutes	Song (3 rotating groups)	'Lord, the light of your love' or 'Colours of Day'
10 minutes	Prayer	Star prayers
30 minutes	Concluding worship	Worship with parents and carers

BASIC RECIPES

PLAY DOUGH

You will need:
- ★ 2 cups plain flour
- ★ 1 cup salt
- ★ 2 tsp cream of tartar
- ★ 2 tbsp cooking oil
- ★ 2 cups boiling water
- ★ Food dye if desired

Mix the flour, salt, cream of tartar and cooking oil together in a bowl. Add two cups of boiling water (just boiled, straight from the kettle). If you want the dough coloured, adding food dye to the water will help the even distribution of colour through the mix. Knead with a hand-held mixer or machine (the dough will be too hot for your hands). Allow the dough to cool (but don't let it crust over) before packing it away in a plastic bag.

BISCUIT MIX

You will need:
- ✩ 300g plain flour (plus extra for flouring surfaces)
- ✩ A pinch of salt
- ✩ 1 tsp baking powder
- ✩ 1 tsp nutmeg and/or 1 tsp ground ginger (if making ginger biscuits)
- ✩ 100g butter or margarine
- ✩ 100g soft brown sugar
- ✩ 2 eggs
- ✩ 60g golden syrup
- ✩ Mixing bowl and spoon or hand-held mixer
- ✩ Baking parchment or greaseproof paper
- ✩ Rolling pins
- ✩ Biscuit cutters
- ✩ Pencils
- ✩ Hand-washing facilities

Put the flour, salt, baking powder and spice into a bowl. Rub in the butter or margarine, then stir in the sugar. Beat the eggs with the golden syrup and add to the mixture. Mix well either by hand or with a hand-held mixer.

Divide the dough into pieces sufficient for each child. Have a surface ready for rolling: pieces of well-floured baking parchment or greaseproof paper on your normal table covering work well and are disposable later. The dough should be rolled out to about 5mm thickness and then the biscuits can be cut out.

Get the children to place their biscuits on a named piece of baking parchment. The biscuits will need to be baked in an oven preheated to Gas Mark 3 or 160°C for about 18 minutes, but keep an eye on them.

BREAD DOUGH

You will need:

- ★ 400g strong plain flour
- ★ 2 level tsp sugar
- ★ 2 level tsp dried yeast (the fast-action variety)
- ★ 1.5 level tsp salt
- ★ 230ml plus 5 tbsp warm water
- ★ 2 tbsp olive oil
- ★ 2 mixing bowls
- ★ Mixing spoon
- ★ Sieve
- ★ Clean tea towel
- ★ Greaseproof paper
- ★ Baking tray
- ★ Cooling rack

Sift the flour, sugar, yeast and salt into a bowl. (If you are using yeast that needs to be reconstituted in water first, follow the instructions on the packet). Add the water and oil and knead well. Cover with a clean tea towel and leave in a warm place for approximately one hour until it has doubled in size.

Turn the dough out on to a floured surface and knead again evenly until smooth. Divide the dough and shape as required. Place finished products on a greased and floured baking tray. Cover with the tea towel and leave until doubled in size.

Bake in the centre of a preheated oven at Gas Mark 5 or 190°C for 45–50 minutes for a loaf and 15–20 minutes for rolls, until they are golden brown and the base sounds hollow when tapped. Cool on a wire rack.

You will need:
- ★ 1–2 tbsp milk
- ★ A few drops peppermint oil
- ★ 250–300g icing sugar (sifted)
- ★ Mixing bowls
- ★ Mixing spoons
- ★ Rolling pin
- ★ Small pastry cutters
- ★ Baking tray
- ★ Greaseproof paper
- ★ Small cardboard gift boxes
- ★ Ribbon

Put the milk in a bowl and add the peppermint oil. Gradually add the icing sugar until a stiff mixture is formed. Turn the mixture out on to greaseproof paper that has been dusted with sifted icing sugar, and roll out to 0.5cm in thickness. Cut into rounds with a small pastry cutter. Gather the trimmings, re-roll and re-cut until all the mixture is used up.

Place sweets on a baking tray lined with greaseproof paper until dry. Have available some small attractive boxes to put the sweets into when they are dry.

Makes approximately 20 sweets.

BASIC CRAFT SKILLS

PREPARING A COLLAGE BOARD

You will need: sheet of MDF board, measuring approximately 600mm x 1000mm, lining wallpaper, masking tape and/or double-sided sticky tape.

Cover the boards with lining wallpaper. The children can then collage straight on to the boards and the finished work can be displayed in the church against a rail or pillar.

Having two collage boards will afford you extra flexibility, as you can keep the children's work on display for longer with one board on display and the other one in the course of preparation.

You will need: a large rectangle of hessian or heavyweight upholstery or curtain fabric, measuring approximately 0.5 metre long by 1 metre wide or to suit the area where you wish to hang it, broom handle or length of dowel or pipe, thick twine or curtain cord, sewing thread and needle or a sewing machine.

Hem round all sides of the fabric. Turn a casing along one of the shorter sides through which the broom handle can be threaded. Attach the twine or curtain cord to the ends of the broom handle and hang the banner from an available hook. Alternatively, omit the casing and pole and hang the banner on a bare wall, using Blu-tack or masking tape to secure in place.

MAKING A FEELY BOX

You will need: small cardboard boxes (half case of wine size is ideal), offcuts of fabric, elastic, scissors, sewing thread and needle, PVA glue.

Cut some fabric to make a sleeve to fit round the open end of the box. Make a casing along one end. Sew or glue the side seam of the fabric, making sure that the sleeve fits around the box and that you can still get to both ends of the casing.

When the glue is dry, thread the casing with elastic, pull it through and tie the ends together so that the elastic expands enough for you to get your hand inside easily, but is tight enough to make it hard to see what is inside. Fit the sleeve over the box and glue in place so that it comes well over the open end of the box.

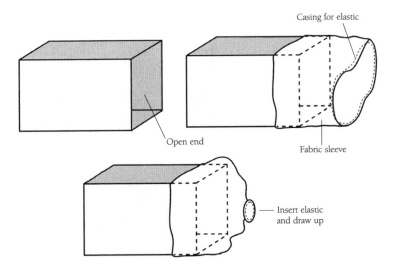

Casing for elastic

Open end

Fabric sleeve

Insert elastic and draw up

TEMPLATES

STAR

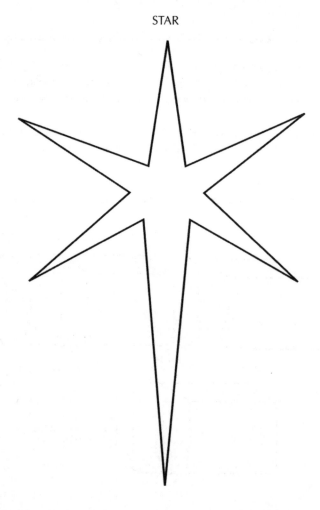

THREE WISE MEN

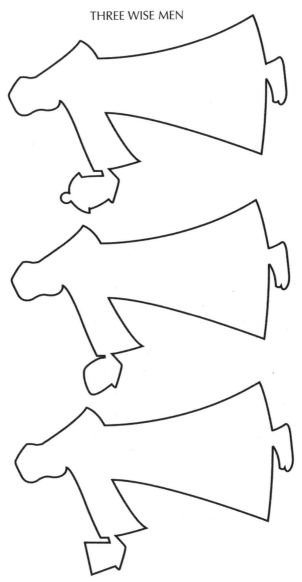

Reproduced with permission from *Not Sunday, Not School!* published by BRF 2006 (1 84101 490 7) **www.barnabasinchurches.org.uk**

CAMEL

BABY JESUS

MARY AND JOSEPH

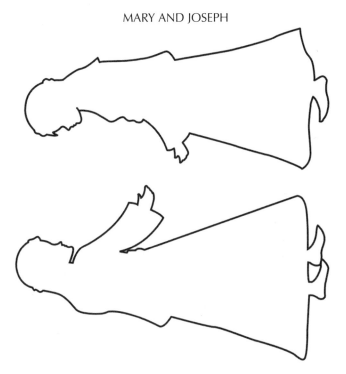

Hen shape; Chick beak and feet

SHEEP SHAPES

FISH SHAPE FOR FISH TANKS AND FISH WHIRLIGIG

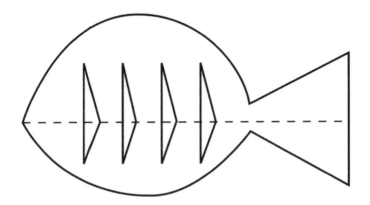

BIBLIOGRAPHY

Listed below are the resources used directly for this book and for the original workshops, as well as those that have provided inspiration and ideas. A wide selection of Bibles in different versions is very useful to find the right translation for a particular story (it won't always be a children's Bible). Alongside Christian material, general activity books and children's storybooks can often be adapted to illustrate a Christian theme.

BIBLES AND BIBLE STORIES

The Dramatised Bible (Marshall Pickering, 1989)
The Lion Children's Bible (Lion, 1981)
International Children's Bible (Nelson Word, 1983)
Contemporary English Version of the Bible (HarperCollins, 2000)
New Revised Standard Version of the Bible (OUP, 1989)
The Children's Illustrated Bible (Dorling Kindersley, 1994)
The Usborne Children's Bible (Usborne, 2000)
My Book of Bible Stories (Lion, 2002)
Stories Jesus Told, Nick Butterworth and Mick Inkpen (Marshall Pickering, 1996)

SONG BOOKS

Junior Praise (Marshall Pickering, 1986)
Hymns Old and New (Kevin Mayhew, 1996)
Kidsource (Kevin Mayhew, 2002)

Godly Play, Jerome W. Berryman (Augsburg, 1991)

Young Children and Worship, Sonya M. Stewart and Jerome W. Berryman (Westminster John Knox Press, 1989)

Following Jesus, Sonya M. Stewart and Jerome W. Berryman (Geneva Press, 2000)

Teaching Godly Play, Sonya M. Stewart and Jerome W. Berryman (Abingdon Press, 1995)

The Complete Guide to Godly Play, Volumes 1–5, Jerome W. Berryman (Living the Good News, 2002)

Theme Games, Lesley Pinchbeck (Scripture Union, 1993)

Theme Games 2, Lesley Pinchbeck (Scripture Union, 2002)

Festive Allsorts: Ideas for Celebrating the Christian Year Nicola Currie (National Society/CHP, 1994)

Seasons and Saints for the Christian Year, Nicola and Stuart Currie (National Society/CHP, 1998)

The 'E' Book: Essential prayers and activities for faith at home, Gill Ambrose (National Society/CHP, 2000)

Children Aloud, Gordon and Ronni Lamont (National Society/CHP, 1997)

One Hundred and One Ideas for Creative Prayers, Judith Merrell (Scripture Union, 1995)

New Ideas for Creative Prayer, Judith Merrell (Scripture Union, 2001)

The Gospels Unplugged, Lucy Moore (BRF, 2002)

The Lord's Prayer Unplugged, Lucy Moore (BRF, 2004)

Here's One I Made Earlier, Kathryn Copsey (Scripture Union, 1995)

Here's Another One I Made Earlier, Christine Orme (Scripture Union, 2000)

Come and Join the Celebration, John Muir and Betty Pedley (National Society/CHP, 2001)

Welcome to the Lord's Table, Margaret Withers (BRF, 1999)

Special Times with God, Anne Faulkner (BRF, 2002)

CHILDREN'S ACTIVITY BOOKS

Festive Fun, Gillian Souter (Off the Shelf Publishing, 2001)
Fun to Make, Gillian Souter (Off the Shelf Publishing, 2001)
Beads and Badges, Gillian Souter (Off the Shelf Publishing, 1999)
Cool Stuff, Susie Lacome (MQ Publications, 2002)
Play Together Learn Together, Melanie Rice (Kingfisher, 1985)
Fun to Make and Do, Hannah Tofts and Annie Owen (Two-Can Publisher, 1990)
Making Presents, Juliet Bawden (Hamlyn Children's Books, 1993)
What Shall I Do Today?, R. Gibson (Usborne)
Make and Colour Paper Planes, Clare Beaton (b small publishing, 2000)
Bible Make and Do, Books 1–4, Gillian Chapman (BRF, 2003)
Christmas Make and Do, Gillian Chapman (BRF, 2004)

OTHER RESOURCES

Bright Star Night, Lois Rock (Lion, 1997)
Jesus' Christmas Party, Nicholas Allan (Hutchinson Children's Books, 1991)
Harry and the Bucketful of Dinosaurs, Ian Whybrow and Adrian Reynolds (David & Charles Children's Books, 1999)
A Choice of Anglo-Saxon Verse, Richard Hamer (Faber and Faber, 1970)
How to Eat: The Pleasures and Principles of Good Food, Nigella Lawson (Chatto & Windus, 1998)

NOT SUNDAY, NOT SCHOOL

Additional material available from
barnabasinchurches@brf.org.uk

Visit **barnabasinchurches@brf.org.uk** for an ever-increasing collection of material to inspire your own children's work, ranging from basic information about how to get started to fresh ways to engage children at festival times.

barnabas

Resourcing children's work in church and school

Simply go to **www.brf.org.uk** and visit the barnabas pages

BRF is a Registered Charity

A Browse our books and buy online in our **bookshop**.

B In the **forum**, join discussions with friends and experts in children's work. Chat through the problems we all face, issues facing children's workers, where-do-I-find… questions and more.

C **Free** easy-to-use downloadable **ideas** for children's workers and teachers. Ideas include:
- Getting going with prayer
- Getting going with drama
- Getting going with the Bible… and much more!

D In **The Big Picture**, you'll find short fun reports on Barnabas training events, days we've spent in schools and churches, as well as expertise from our authors, and other useful articles.

E In the section on **Godly Play**, you'll find a general introduction and ideas on how to get started with this exciting new approach to Christian education.